MW00441218

WANDERING HOME

WANDERING HOME

TOM RODDY

Illustrations by Kyle Brooks

Published by Looking Glass Books, Inc.
Decatur, Georgia

ISBN: 978-1-929619-51-1
Manufactured in the United States of America

Contents

Spring

Summer

Acknowledgments

Thank you, thank you, thank you, people.

My mom, Mary Lois Wright Roddy, who affirmed my looking at the world from an atypical perspective. My dad, Pat Roddy Jr., who wrote out his speeches and made them short—including the one to his employees when the Teamsters staged an unauthorized strike.

J. P. Roddy, my grandfather Pop Pops, who let me explore his farm—every barn, old house, field, and copse. It gave me a sense of freedom and adventure. What new world was around the bend and down the road?

Bob Lupton, whose reflections on living in the inner city gave me the inspiration to write about my experiences. My faculty advisor at Columbia Theological Seminary, President Davison Phillips, who was the first person who told me I could write.

Greg Simmons, who came up with the idea of an atypical foundation whose assets were its contacts, not its bank account. Judge Frank Eldridge, who was a superior court judge in Fulton County, Georgia. The board of Atlanta Resource Foundation and especially Billy Mitchell, a commercial real estate developer, who stayed after me until I finished this project.

Barbara Thompson, who read, edited, encouraged, cajoled, and redlined hundreds of pages. But most important, she believed in me and revved me up when I went blank.

Alexandra, my wife, my chief cheerleader, who finally figured me out and still loves me.

If I have forgotten you, I want to collectively thank you. Pat U Self.

Introduction

For more than thirty years I presided over a nonorganization organization called the Atlanta Resource Foundation. Our major work was to encourage people who in many different ways were bringing hope to people living in Atlanta's most difficult neighborhoods.

It was hard to explain to people what we did. "But what do you *really* do?" I heard that a lot.

We tried putting together a trifold brochure about our work with real life stories, but it was costly and burdensome. Then I started writing a "nonnews" newsletter about what was going on in the city and also inside of me—as I came up against the promises and demands of the gospel and the stark realities and disparities of urban life. Friends began telling me that they looked forward to these reflections because they were off the wall.

"We still don't know what you do, but you should publish your stories!"

Wandering Home is that book. Some of the details (why and when, who did what) have been left out to make it easier for readers unfamiliar with Atlanta to make sense of the material. Some situations will seem familiar to people who have walked together with me through the years. Journeying together in one city for many decades, we have seen that history repeats itself. The same personalities and the same issues keep popping back up. There are economic booms and busts, the ongoing displacement of the poor, rising rhetoric around immigrants, and the pull of a retaliatory response to terrorism.

When Atlanta won the 1996 Summer Olympics, we were involved in the redevelopment of neighborhoods adjacent to the new Olympic Stadium. We helped mobilize the faith community to welcome visitors to Atlanta. We created the Summerhill Neighborhood Redevelopment Association and launched Quest Atlanta. Through it all we could never escape the plight of the poor, especially the homeless.

During our years together, we lost two of our strongest visionaries, Emmit Young and Greg Simmons, in horrible accidents. We also lost two of our wisdom figures to cancer—Dr. Lawrence Bottoms, former moderator of the Presbyterian Church (U.S.A.), and Rev. Raynell Perkins, an associate rector at St. Luke's Presbyterian Church.

On the morning of September 11, 2001, at a community-wide breakfast with Marian Wright Edelman, we launched an ecumenical movement. We were strategizing how to give at-risk children a healthy start when terrorists began their attacks on the World Trade Center and the Pentagon.

In spite of the pressures on us to march to the increased pace of a city that has doubled in size, we have tried to organize our lives around the four seasons and the diurnal clock, as did our forebears for so many hundreds of years. Like our children and grandchildren, we begin our year in the fall. In the winter we bundle up, huddle down, and long for spring, when our hopeful waiting is realized. In the summer, we try to relax but stay alert, so that we are not tripped up by the unexpected that unexpectedly happens.

So our journey begins.

Getting on the Road

Gandalf: You ought to go and you ought to go soon.
Frodo: What about the autumn, on or after my
birthday?
I think I could make some arrangements by then....

It's not easy to take to an unknown road. Like Frodo in J. R. R. Tolkien's *Lord of the Rings*, I have a million excuses for not setting out. I am not ready. The timing is bad. It might be dangerous. There is no guide, no companion. It might not even be the right road.

When I was in high school, I worked during the summer for my father at a manufacturing and distributing plant in Knoxville, Tennessee. I apprenticed for almost every job, including sweeping and cleaning, loading and delivery, and machine repair. Dad liked to get on the road by 6:15 a.m. so he could open up for the early delivery drivers. I was a teenager running on a late-night biological clock, and virtually every morning, it took a Herculean effort to get up and get going.

As an adult, it's even harder to get on the road. There are bills to pay. Letters to write. People calling with their emergencies. Travel plans. What should I take? How can I lighten up? By the time I leave, there are so many things hanging from my body, it's hard to move. Camera, cell phone with earpiece, pouch with ID and ticket, gadget watch that has ceased to gadget, glasses. When I get to security, I have to take it all off and then find everything again. Better to stay home, plop down with a good book, turn on the computer....

But there is the call of the road, the urgent invitation. The road as a metaphor for the spiritual journey is as old as Abraham and as current as the movie adaptations of Lord of the Rings. Gandalf's stern message to Frodo rings true:

> And you must go, or at least set out, either North,
> South, East or West.

The journey may involve getting on a real road—moving our feet—or a metaphorical pilgrimage. But it always involves a journey of our soul. Yahweh says to Abraham, "Get thee out of thy father's house to a land which I will show thee." In Jewish literature, the happy person is the one who has found the right road, who doesn't walk in the way of the ungodly. Jesus calls his disciples to go on a journey. When he passes by Levi *sitting,* he says, "Follow me." Get on the road.

Here's what I tell myself when I am having trouble getting on the road:

The way will be shown. Which way? How will I know the road to take? We would never get on the road if we knew its true direction, its length, or its dangers. So it's good to have a short-range goal. For Frodo, Rivendell, the land of the elves, was a doable goal—although that road would be fraught with more adventure and peril than he expected. At Rivendell, the next road would be revealed.

Gandalf: But you cannot see very far; neither can I.

Frodo: But in the meantime what course am I to take?

Gandalf: Towards danger, but not too rashly, nor too straight...make for Rivendell. That journey should not prove too perilous, though the Road is less easy than it was, and it will grow worse as the year fails.

Frodo: Rivendell! Very good. I will go East and I will make for Rivendell.

There will be companions. I would go, but the road will be lonely. I have no one to go with me. Why leave the companionship of wife and children and the warmth of a crackling fire for the uncertainties of solitary travel on a foreign road?

Young Frodo resolved to go alone, but unexpectedly three of his hobbit friends joined him. As the road lengthened and the dangers increased, he was given another companion—a mysterious scout, a fierce warrior king in disguise, with thousands at his command.

The way will be hard. But that is life. Jesus tells us that the way to life is narrow and rocky. Muscles must be used and even stressed, or they will atrophy. The soul that is untested never develops endurance.

The trail is a loop. I'll never get back? Not necessarily. The best trails are loops, although only the adventurous plan a loop from the beginning. It is much easier and more certain to go back the way we came. Out and back. But eventually, if the journey is successful, there will be a loop, and we will get back home. While on their journey, Frodo and his friends sang:

> Home is behind, the world ahead
> And here are many paths to tread
> Through shadows to the edge of night,
> Until the stars are all alight.
> Then world behind and home ahead,
> We'll wander back to home and bed.

"You can never go home again" is true if it means that home always changes. On our most important journeys, we come home changed, and we become agents of change. Frodo and his fellow travelers eventually come back to the Shire. But they left sneaking out at night, and they return riding on horses, decorated as grownup heroes and agents of the king.

There is reward. Fellow travelers are transformed by the road and become a trusted team. As they grow, they are able to help others. They are not just *in* history; they *make* history. The way of the poor in spirit, the meek, and the weak triumphs over the power of evil, and all middle earth blooms and flourishes again.

We will never know what contribution we make to history through our little journey unless we get on the road. It is fall. September is gone. October is flying by. Thanksgiving will soon be here. The leaves are falling. It is time to get on the road.

Forward Home

Sunday afternoon in the mountains,
rainy and overcast.
In an hour or so we pack and leave.
It is the last Sunday of August.

In two days September will begin.
All my grandchildren have gone back to school.
My daughter-in-law has left for her graduate program.
The dining room of the inn is empty.
An Anglican service was beautiful,
but only one person knows our name.

Is there an August sadness embedded in the soul?
I've had twenty-two of them to get ready for school.
It started early.
Get up, Tommy. Get dressed, Tommy.
Get your notebook. You will be late.
Eat your cereal. Eat your eggs.
You will need the energy.

The days shorten.
The darkness lengthens.
My inner voice barks commands:
Get in shape for football.
Finish required reading.
Pack for military school.
Up at reveille.

Shirt and tie at last call.
Papers are due.
Exams are coming.

Primitive voices call out:
The play of summer is over.
Harvest is here.
Winter is coming.
Prepare for cold, the scourge of flu, hunger, and the Darkness.

But wait! The harvest is joyous, a feast.
Fresh winds blow.
The cool nip of autumn revives the spirit.
Trees bear lush fruit, full of summer rain.
Squirrels store away their winter meals.

The creation is not sad.
It stands on tiptoe awaiting the harvest.

We don't fall back into September; we go forward to fall.
We don't go back home but forward to home.
The best is still ahead.

Where Were You on September 11, 2001?

There are two ways of remembering. One is to make
an excursion from the living present back to the dead
past. The other way is to summon the dead past into
the living present. The young widow remembers
her husband, and he is there beside her. When Jesus
said, "Do this in remembrance of me," he was not
prescribing a slug of nostalgia.

—Fredrick Buechner, *Wishful Thinking, A Theological ABC*

It is Tuesday morning, the 11th of September 2001. Alexandra
and I are attending a prayer breakfast in downtown Atlanta
with some friends working in the inner city. An imam, a rabbi,
a priest, and a pastor lead us in reading Scripture. We pray for
the innocent children trapped in poverty in our city and state
and world. A children's choir performs. They are boys and girls
from many different nationalities and races, their faces bright
and innocent.

A plane from Boston to Los Angeles makes a sharp
unauthorized turn south toward New York City.

Andrew Young takes the podium. He is an American legend,
homegrown in Atlanta—a civil rights movement hero, ambassador, mayor, member of Congress, and peacemaker. He introduces Marian Wright Edelman, a graduate of Atlanta's Spelman
College and the founder and leader of the Children's Defense
Fund. She is a tireless advocate for children.

A second plane traveling from Boston's Logan Airport
to Los Angeles makes a sharp, unauthorized turn
toward New York City.

Dr. Edelman challenges us to take seriously the needs of millions of poor children across the United States. She tells us one in five children lives in poverty. A high percentage of urban poor children will end up in the justice system. Most poor children in America are white rural kids. But it is possible to give a healthy start, a head start, a fair start, a safe start, and a moral start to every child in America. Dr. Edelman's passion makes believers of us all.

The World Trade Center is hit by an airplane. Then a
second plane hits.

A cell phone rings, and someone whispers to Ambassador Young. He quickly leaves. We are sent forth with a song: "We Shall Overcome." My wife and I stroll to our car, stopping to greet friends along the way. There's a long line of cars waiting to exit the garage. Many people are talking on their phones.

American Airlines Flight 77 hits the Pentagon south wall.

We stop at a post office to buy stamps. The atmosphere behind the counter is somber. I hear frantic conversation among the postal workers and ask what's going on. "You need to go home and turn on your television. The World Trade Center has been hit by hijackers."

Where were you on September 11? Until that day, I regarded the question "Where were you when x happened to y?" as just a conversation piece. I mean, what does it matter where you were unless you were standing next to y?

But what if the reason we keep asking this seemingly inane question is that it is not inane? Perhaps where we are when great historical events happen has some profound, albeit hidden significance, even if only for our own lives.

Tuesday morning, September 11, 2001. I am with my wife and some friends in the presence of an imam, a rabbi, a priest, and a pastor. Not my usual company. We each approach religious faith and helping the poor in different ways, but on this day, we are united by a concern for children. We have come together to pray for not only the children of America but of the world. We learn that children can be helped if we give them loving care and the tools they need for a healthy start.

Over the years, the message of that September 11, 2001, prayer breakfast has been filed away in the dusty archives of my memory. It was eclipsed by the fireball explosions and the collapse of the World Trade Center towers. Perhaps now is the time to dig it out of the rubble, to pull from the seared place of my memory the challenge to care for children. Children who cannot speak for themselves.

I want to remember that on September 11, 2001, we were challenged as Muslims, Christians, and Jews to work hand in hand, shoulder to shoulder. I want to hear again the children of many races singing "We Shall Overcome." I want to remember the words of Jesus:

Anyone who welcomes one little child like this in my name welcomes me. But anyone who is the downfall of one of these little ones who have faith in me would be better drowned in the depths of the sea with a great millstone round his neck.

I wonder what else, who else I can summon from that dead past into the living present, my present. What can I do that honors history and compels us toward a brighter, less violent future?

Where were you on September 11, 2001? Is there something, someone from that experience that you want to bring into the living present?

I Hate You

Father, forgive them for they do not know what they
are doing.

— Jesus of Nazareth

It is one of the hardest things for me to handle after the terrorist
attacks of September 11, 2001. There are people who hate me,
my family, my friends, my fellow Americans, and the family of
human beings that I belong to around the globe. They are plot-
ting right now to get you and me.

They may not know my name, but they know me in general
terms. I am black, white, Latino, Asian, Arab, Native American.
I am a citizen or an immigrant, legal or illegal, a southerner or
a northerner. It makes no difference. I live in the United States;
therefore, to them I am Babylon. I deserve destruction.

Before September 11, someone writing such things might
have been considered paranoid. Maybe we should have been a
little more paranoid.

September 1942. It is recess time on my first day at my
new school. I am in the first grade, and my daddy is going off
to World War II. I walk down the steps toward the playground.
Some kid yells, "Let's get the new guys!" It turns out there are two
of us. Jimmy Anderson and me.

Jimmy looks at me and stutters, "Ru-run for da' hi-high gr-
ground. We'll fi-fight 'em off there." How did I get in this fight?
Why should anyone dislike the new guys? I thought we were
fighting the Japanese.

At the high end of the playground, with our backs to the corner of the fence, Corregidor style, we make our last stand against the hordes of attackers. Jimmy has a pretty good right cross, so there are kids on the ground. But it's not Jimmy's punch that saves us. It's the piercing whistle of our principal.

October 1952. I am in high school playing football. We are the scrubs, playing the B- team of our crosstown rival. This is not Friday night football with bands, cheerleaders, and screaming fans. This is a weekday afternoon. They come over in their little blue bus for a scrimmage game.

On the kickoff, I am surprised when I am hit late by a guy growling at me like some kind of wild animal. On the next offensive play, he comes at me again, still growling. The run is on the other side of the field, but he is not playing the game. He is just trying to hurt me. I look in his eyes and see rage. I recognize him; he is a neighbor. But what could he have against me? Why does he hate me?

The next few times he comes growling at me, I go under him, knock him off his feet, and send him sprawling. Then I go on playing the game. He grows tired of growling and leaves me alone.

November 1953. I am a reserve linebacker on the varsity team. The coach drafts me to play offensive halfback on the dummy squad impersonating the team that we will play Friday night in our biggest game of the season. He even gives me a jersey, number 21. I will be the opposition halfback in scrimmage all week. "You are to live, eat, and run like this guy," my coach orders.

The humiliation of being used as fodder is overcome by the thrill of getting my hands on the ball. I am a bit obnoxious, suggesting I am going to run the ball down the first team's throats. Their defense lets me off lightly, barely roughing me up.

During the real game I surprise myself. Yelling from the sidelines, I taunt and jeer at the real number 21 every chance I get. He ignores me and plays on. My coach shoots me an agitated look. *What have I created?* "Shut up! You are going to get us penalized." I never do get in the game, and my hate-filled name calling from the sideline accomplishes nothing. We are thoroughly beaten.

Fast-forward to the late 1960s. I am in a Latin American high school, translating for a talented gospel quartet from the States. Anti-U.S. feeling runs high among the students, and some of them behave rudely, chanting "Yankee, go home!" We cut the program short. As I leave, I tell a group of students, "I hope when you visit my country, my people will not treat you like you have treated me." (As an aside: Now thousands upon thousands of their children are in our U.S. schools, and I am wondering, *Are they being treated any better than I was?*)

Here's the point: If we are alive, we are going to pick up some enemies sometime, somewhere. Yes, real enemies, enemies who dislike us for no apparent reason. We can plot to get even. We can target their leaders like they have targeted ours. We can even try to understand why they hate us, but right now we must dodge their attacks.

In the end, however, it is not hate that wins. Hate will never win. Hate creates its little side game, but it is not the real game. *Hate-filled people are sideline people.* We have to stay in the game. Stay focused. In case we are feeling a little lonely, a little unappreciated and picked on, we are in good company "They hated me without cause," said Jesus of Nazareth. With cause and without cause, as individuals and as representatives of groups and even countries, we are going to be hated. We will have to learn to live with it.

But how?

Excellent instruction on how to live with hate comes from the teachings of Jesus and the words he spoke to his disciples just before his crucifixion. You can read these for yourself in John 13 through 17. Jesus is preparing his disciples for his departure. He wants to give them tools for dealing with the hatred that will inevitably come at them when they attempt to work for peace, when they attempt to live by loving, when they pray for and forgive their enemies.

With these tools, it might even be possible for us to pray for, ask a blessing on, and sometimes even love those who hate us.

Father, forgive them for they do not know what they are doing.

Living with Hatred

Company. You are in good company. Jesus said: They hated me. They will hate you. They hated me without cause, and they will hate you without cause. But there is a fellowship of those who are hated and hurt by others. We are in it together.

Comfort. Jesus said that he would send his Spirit, the one called alongside, to be with us in all places and in all times, 24/7. The original Greek word means attorney, helper, comforter, advocate.

Conviction. Our advocate will sort out the right from the wrong, truth from lies, and judge fairly. We will tire of vindictive prayers. We will learn to pray in the Spirit for more than just what we ourselves want for our lives and the people we love.

Continue. We will not be removed from the suffering of the world, but Jesus is praying to his Father for our protection, our continuance.

Call to Mind. The Spirit will remind us what Jesus taught and guide us into knowing the truth. The Spirit will help us apply Jesus's teachings to our situation.

(Anti)Terrorists

They work in groups of twos and threes.
Live simply.
Are not encumbered with many possessions.
Depend totally upon one another.
Make binding commitments.
Form alliances with others for specific objectives.

They have jobs that are not their real jobs.
Learn specific skills and share them with their
comrades.
Are able to pick up and move quickly.
Don't waste many words in idle talk.

They are multilingual.
Able to move quietly across borders.
They expect and receive hospitality from comrades.
Communicate quickly, quietly, clandestinely.
Don't want publicity or credit.

They think globally but act locally.
Are willing to die for their cause.
Endure present hardships for eternal awards.
Are committed to one man.

These are the agents of a new, revolutionary kingdom.
They destroy their enemies by loving them.
They are motivated by love for their leader.
They live by only two commands:

Love God with all your heart, mind, and soul.
Love your neighbor as yourself.

Names, please.
Martha and Mary
Peter, James, and John
Priscilla and Aquila
Paul and Barnabas
And hundreds and thousands through the ages who
follow the radical from Galilee.
Who only want to please him.
Who destroy terror, fear, and hopelessness.

What Networking Cannot Do

Repentance is no fun at all. It is something much harder than merely eating humble pie. It means unlearning all the self-conceit and self-will that we have been training ourselves into for thousands of years. It means killing a part of yourself, undergoing a kind of death....

Remember, this repentance, this willing submission to humiliation and a kind of death, is not something God demands of you before he will take you back and which he could let you off if he chose; it is simply a description of what going back to him is like. If you ask God to take you back without it, you are really asking him to let you go back without going back. It cannot happen.

—C. S. Lewis, *Mere Christianity*

I am attending a high-profile tea, talking to a young lady who is there to network with important community leaders. She thanks me for my monthly letters from the Atlanta Resource Foundation, but she is clearly puzzled. "What is it you *do*?" I try to explain that, among other things, I help organizations working with poor people in the city to maximize their skills and resources by connecting them with each other and with people who can offer them practical and professional help.

This only confuses her more. "But what do you do *right now*?"

I mentally browse my needs list. Aha! "Right now, I need a person with heating and air conditioning skills to help a ministry to homeless people. They have an old, inefficient system, and they need to know how to heat their nursery without heating their whole building." It turns out she knows someone who knows someone, and before long the problem is solved.

When I was growing up, if people had told me that they were networking, I would have thought that they were getting ready for a fishing trip. Now, connecting individuals and organizations to the help they need is a gift and talent that takes up most of my time. It is not as sterile and professional as a referral. I might not be able to solve your problem, but maybe I know someone who can. And, by the way, you will need to treat them right. Help them feel that they are making an important contribution, and give them the opportunity to connect with people in your circle. Thank them and thank them again. Pay them what you can, even if it is a plate of brownies.

Networking. It's great!

But wait. A nonprofit leader tells me there is a situation that she doesn't know how to handle. A small group of people who originally welcomed her ministry has turned on it. She has tried everything to make peace, to accommodate the demands of the person who heads the offending organization. "It appears that the only way to satisfy him is to leave and give him the key to the building," she tells me with frustration and anger.

This is harder, but my networking mind starts scanning the database. I know someone who knows the problematic leader. I send my friend to talk with him. No change. I send a new person, then another. No one is changing. No one is talking. The network is not working.

Then it is Lent. I am thinking that Lent is about eating and drinking less, praying, looking a little sorrowful. I have forgotten that it is about repentance, and first of all, about personal repentance. *Against thee and thee only have I sinned,* the psalmist confesses. My pastor tells the congregation that the Spirit will remind us about people we have offended. People we need to forgive and people from whom we need to ask forgiveness.

Oh no, not him! Forgive this guy who is trying to shut down a shelter, apparently for personal gain? Lord? You want me…? I do not like the way this is going. God is getting personal with me. He is not affirming. He is pointing out the dirt. I do not know where this is headed.

But I do know that I cannot help you change your enemy. I have no one to send you who can do that. And I am in the same boat. I cannot change how my enemy feels about me. I can only change how I feel about my enemy. I can only change myself—something networking cannot do.

A Little Tiff About Forgiveness

Am I not destroying my enemies when I make friends of them?

—Abraham Lincoln

Tonight, you and I were having an interesting discussion about settling little tiffs when we got into a little tiff. Before I knew it, it was a full-blown argument. One of our disagreements was about forgiveness. You said, "I hate her." I said, "Forgiveness is the only way to get free from her." You disagreed. How could you not see my point? I did not take my own advice about settling little tiffs. Instead, I became angry and stomped away.

I apologize and ask for your forgiveness.

As part of my penance, here are some thoughts on forgiveness, on why I need to keep working at it, even when, in small matters and large, it can be one of the hardest steps I ever take. I try to forgive because...

I don't want to be stuck. People who do not forgive are time stuck. They are forced, even against their will, to relive the past, to go over and over again in their minds events that are ten, twenty, even fifty years old. So much of their attention, creativity, energy, and zeal are directed backward that they cannot keep up with what is happening now. The war, terror, and oppression taking place between Israelis and Palestinians today is just one of many stark examples. There are people destroying the present because they are trying to change something that happened in the past.

God is a judge. I'm not; God is. My act of forgiveness does not absolve anyone from his or her sins. They have to seek God for absolution. But my forgiveness does release the Spirit of God to work in the spirit of the person who has wounded me. "Whatever you bind on earth shall be bound in heaven, and whatever you loose on earth shall be loosed in heaven."[1]

I have heroic examples. There are people just like you and me who have been able to forgive the most horrific offenses. One of my favorite examples is Corrie ten Boom. She and her family were arrested by the Germans in occupied Holland because they were hiding Jewish citizens. She was sent to Ravensbrück concentration camp along with her sister and father, both of whom suffered terribly in prison and died from the cruel treatment of their captors.

After the war, Corrie became a powerful force for reconciliation, writing and speaking about the need for forgiveness. Her greatest test came when she was invited to speak in postwar Germany. A stout, aging German came up to her and said that he had been a guard at the Ravensbrück camp. He held out his hand and asked for forgiveness. Corrie recognized him as the guard who had been so cruel to her sister Betsie, and specific scenes of his cruelty flashed before her eyes. I will let you read her book *The Hiding Place* to understand how hard it was for her to forgive and the release and freedom it gave her when she was finally able to do it. If someone like Corrie ten Boom can forgive so much, surely I can forgive a little.

In some mysterious way, God's forgiveness of me depends on my forgiveness of others. I learned this from a conversation that Jesus was having with his best friends. He

---

1   Matthew 18:18.

told them to forgive others as they themselves were forgiven for their own sins. "For if you forgive people their trespasses, your heavenly Father will forgive you; but if you do not forgive people their trespasses, neither will your Father forgive your trespasses." Many people have tried to explain these words; I can't. But they have the ring of truth.

I have to forgive again and again, because the first time doesn't usually clean out all the resentment and hurt. It's like getting rid of crabgrass from the lawn. Just when you think it's gone, more pops up. Roots remain. Pull up the roots again, again, and again.

I forgive because I'm asked to forgive, because it sets me free, because I have hurt others and I, too, need forgiveness. I need to forgive whether I feel like it or not, and most often I don't feel like it. If I'm lucky, feeling follows fact. When Jesus taught his closest followers to pray, "Forgive us our debts as we forgive our debtors," he doesn't mention the need to *feel* love or forgiveness in our hearts. Just do it. Do it now. Do it quickly.

Trail Signs

The sun is going down, but there is time for a short, brisk walk before dark. It is going to be my last chance to talk with my wife, Alexandra, before I leave for a two-week trip to Brazil. I will be visiting four cities, spending time with friends from many different political and social backgrounds. Some are members of Parliament, and some work with Brazil's five million abandoned children.

I sense some unsettledness between Alexandra and me, and I invite her to come with me to one of my favorite Atlanta hiking spots, the Chattahoochee River Trail. "You'll love it," I tell her. "The path is level, and there's a great breeze coming off the water."

We take Bootsie, our animated, friend-making Lhasa, and park at the trailhead. I notice there are a lot more people and dogs returning to their cars than starting out. Twenty minutes into our walk, I see that Alexandra is falling behind.

"Are we going back soon?" she asks. "I'm pretty tired."

I am just getting warmed up.

"I'll run ahead and up the hill trail, and you can wait for me here or loop back to the parking lot," I explain quickly. "I'll catch up with you. Ten minutes max."

Later I learn that Alexandra cannot see the place where the hill trail starts. I forgot the first rule of the trail: give simple instructions, ask for feedback, and create a backup plan.

I run up the short path of the hill trail and then head back to the main trail. Alexandra is nowhere to be seen. Assuming that she is looping back to the car, I run toward the parking lot. I

FALL

cannot see her anywhere. I head back to the trail, running faster. I dart up side trails and backtrack on all the possible routes that she might have taken. It's December and already dusk. The winter darkness is coming on quickly.

"Have you seen a blonde lady with a little Lhasa?" I ask the few remaining hikers. No one has seen her.

I had forgotten the second rule of the trail: never leave someone alone on their first time out.

I run back to the car and see that Alexandra is still not there. My heart sinks. "I've lost my wife, and I don't know what to do," I tell a passing stranger. He gives me two quarters, enough to make two phone calls. The phone eats the first quarter. I insert the second quarter and call home. The phone rings and rings. Nuts! I hear my voice on the answering machine and leave a message.

Now it is very dark. I run back up the trail. I stop a young man on a mountain bike. He does not want to help but finally gives in. He, too, covers all the possible routes back to the parking lot. "Now I am going home," he announces.

I drive the car past the barricade onto the trail. I'll risk arrest, keep my high beams on until I see someone. A couple walks into the light, and I hail them. "Have you seen a lady and a little dog?" They have covered the trail from one end to the other, and they have not seen anyone. "There's no one else there," they assure me.

I turn around and drive back to the parking lot. A man is waiting for me. "I am not going to leave you. I am driving out on that trail." He comes back alone. "You go to the service station," he commands. "Call home. Then call the police and come back here. I'll wait on you."

Rule three of the trail: get help.

In the meantime, Alexandra has arrived at a parking lot, but it is the wrong one. She does not know that there are two parking lots—the south lot where we parked and the north lot where she is waiting for me. She understood me to say, "Keep walking. The trail will make a loop, and I'll catch up with you." Now she is cold, scared, and lost. She stays put.

Fourth rule of the trail: when lost, stay where you are; let people find you.

Alexandra asks for help from two professional women who, like the priest in the story of the Good Samaritan, pass by on the other side. "That's what the rangers are for," they tell her as they walk away. "Let them handle this." Finally, a woman from India, a foreigner, stops to help. "I'll stay with you until we find a park ranger," she says.

By now it has been dark for over an hour. We have given up all hope of finding each other. We have become characters in a *Reader's Digest* story with the last page unwritten.

Eventually my wife and the Indian lady catch sight of a ranger. He calls our home, and my daughter answers. She tells him to take her mother to the south parking lot where I am waiting.

We find each other and learn that the other is all right. There is a good bit of "Why did you leave me?" and "How could I be so misunderstood?" We air our emotions and then take stock of the parable we have just lived. "What's going on here?"

It seems clear that this misadventure on a late Sunday afternoon hike is a warning, an important signal about where we are on our journey together. What trail signs am I missing? I assume that I can walk with my wife on the path of life for a while and then run off and do my thing. I can pop back and she will be waiting there, where I told her to be. She assumes that I know how alone she feels on the trail.

After some soul-searching, I say, "I don't think I should run off to Brazil tomorrow. Perhaps we could wait until we can go together."

I call my friend in Brasilia and tell him the story. "Come when you can come together," he says.

I stay home, and Alexandra and I have two of the most significant weeks of our year. We take a lot of walks, some on the trail, some off. We plan our next trip to Brazil. We are content to be with one another, a confirmation that this time we have read the trail signs right.

What signs do you see along the trail you are on? What do they say about the direction you are going?

Lost Things, Lost People

On November 16, 2001, Atlanta's Hartsfield International Airport shut down for three hours while authorities searched for an unidentified man who broke through security. The man ran down the up escalator reserved for arriving passengers. He was described as a white male wearing a University of Georgia T-shirt.

It had been just two months since 9/11, and authorities feared the worst. The airport was shut down and evacuated. All flights in and out were stopped. People were trapped in the midst of travel, and some had to wait days to get to their destination. AirTran alone estimated its losses in the tens of millions of dollars.

We soon learned the story. The guilty person was not a terrorist but Michael Lasseter, a Georgia football fan taking his son to see the University of Georgia play Ole Miss. As they were about to board their plane, he noticed his video camera was missing. He told his son to get on the plane. He would quickly retrace his steps back to security and return before the plane took off.

Unfortunately, his search took him outside security, and when he tried to reenter, he realized he had left his ticket with his son. According to one witness, a frenzied man in a Georgia T-shirt asked several airline employees for assistance. He was told to get back in line. Some witnesses said he then asked security for help. No luck.

Next he supposedly ran by two security guards (a charge

he later denied) and then down the up escalator. When he was finally apprehended, he said he was not a criminal but a frantic father trying to get to his son. Losing something can mess up your day and other people's day too.

I am not as ready as some to throw the book at Lasseter. I remember the time I lost a camera. It was in the late sixties, and I was a counselor at a college seminar in Washington, DC. My responsibilities included looking out for a number of students. The hotel was large, and it was hard to keep up with everyone. I was looking for one of my students, a bright kid, editor of the paper, long hair, from the University of Miami. I was almost at his room when I remembered that I had left my camera in a seminar room.

✦ ☿ ✦

I ran back through the hall and down the stairs to the terrace and the seminar room. No camera. I pursued hotel personnel through the labyrinth of service corridors. "Have you seen a camera?"

"No see camera. Check with lost and found."

I ran past the conference coordinator. "Where are your students?" he asked in alarm.

"I lost my camera!" I yelled. I breezed by as if he would understand that my camera was more important than any of my kids. I never found my camera, and it had some good pictures in it too.

But whatever happened to my kids? I wrote one and got a good letter back. I never heard from the editor. I lost some valuable time with him, but unlike Michael Lasseter, I really don't know the consequences of my actions.

Like most of us, I have spent irreplaceable, sometimes frantic time looking for lost things—car keys, glasses, cell phones, PalmPilot, lost checks, and lost documents. My searching has taken time from my family and other people. To tell the truth, I have no idea who I ran by in the hall or who I left at the gate.

There is a bit of Michael Lasseter in us all.

I asked some of my friends, "What would you have to forget at a security checkpoint to run back and leave your child with the possibility of making a plane trip without you?"

"I wouldn't do it for any camera," one answered.

I kept upping the ante. "What if you left x or y?"

The choice between possessions and people. If we were asked to decide straight up, there would be no choice. But we never put the question this starkly when we become frantic looking for something we've lost. We are hardly aware that we might be leaving some*one* precious and irreplaceable for some-*thing* valuable but replaceable. We'll be right back.

✦ ☿ ✦

Recently I lost my cell phone. Or rather I misplaced it and didn't remember where I put it. After retracing my steps, my laying-down-places, and enlisting the help of everyone who came into the house, I did something unusual. I said, "I'm not going to let this ruin Christmas. I've got to let it go and go on." I expected that, after the holiday, I would have to go to the mobile phone store and plead for a new phone.

A week later our four-year-old grandson, whose house shares a trail with ours, ate lunch with Alexandra and me. Between bites of a peanut-butter-and-honey sandwich, he said casually, "I found an old cell phone on the trail."

"What did you do with it?" I asked, holding down my excitement.

"My dad told me to throw it away. It was no good." (Dad was thinking the phone was an old one of his.)

"Where did you throw it?"

"In the wastebasket."

We found the wastebasket, and my phone was there. It was good and had twelve messages that were received while resting in the woods under some leaves. My callers seemed to enjoy my story even though I called them back a week late.

I know that with my history I am destined to leave and lose some*thing* else. But it helps to remember this story with such a surprise happy ending.

✦ ☖ ✦

We are at the gate of a new era now. Something is about to be born. It is Advent in the first part of the new millennium. There is a stirring in unexpected places not unlike the stirring that occurred when Jesus was born in Bethlehem during the first census of Caesar Augustus. It was important then for Joseph to stay with Mary and not run off looking for lost things, for a missed opportunity or better accommodations. He might have missed the birth of Jesus altogether.

So now it is important for us to stay with our spouse, our kids, the significant people in our lives and not chase after lost things and opportunities.

Wake up, and strengthen the things that remain, which were about to die; for I have not found your deeds completed in the sight of my God.[2]

2   Revelation 3:2.

Breathe In, Breathe Out

It's Sunday afternoon. I am with my sister at the bedside of her husband, Jess. On the previous Tuesday, Jess had both knees replaced, and by now he should be getting better. But Jess's breathing is high and rapid. The oxygen-uptake monitor has fallen dangerously low, and the doctor thinks he has pneumonia.

"Breathe deeper. Breathe from the diaphragm," we tell him. We take deep breaths ourselves. We pull our arms up and out in a relaxed wave, two soaring birds trying to coax him into deeper breaths.

On Monday we transfer Jess to a hospital better equipped to handle lung disease. The pulmonologist tells us that he has adult pulmonary distress syndrome. "I wish it *were* pneumonia," he says. "We can only support the body and hope that the lungs eventually heal themselves." It takes several days for the seriousness of Jess's illness to sink in. His chest rises and falls with difficulty. When his oxygen level dips below 90 percent, the monitor beeps like a car alarm. I want to breathe for him.

As a way to calm myself and as a form of prayer, I concentrate on my own breathing. I think about how all the world's great religions emphasize the spiritual quality of breath and of slow, deep breathing. The Latin word *spiritus* means breath. Respiration (*re* plus *spiritus*) is the process of inhaling air into the lungs, exchanging oxygen for the carbon dioxide in the blood, and exhaling the stale air. Respiration is *re-spiriting*.

Now, feeling anxious about Jess, I breathe deeply and say a prayer. I meditate and drift into dreams where I see:

God scooping dirt from the ground and forming Man. God breathes into his nostrils the breath of life, and a piece of clay becomes a living being that breathes.[3]

Elijah pleading with God for the life of a poor widow's child. "My God, I pray let this child's soul [breath] come back to him." The boy revives, and the prophet carries the boy to his mother.[4]

The prophet Ezekiel, disillusioned by the calamity that has fallen upon his country. He has a vision of a vast valley full of dry bones. It is a hopeless, discouraging sight, especially when he learns that the bones represent his people. The prophet speaks, and there is the sound of rattling bones being pieced together. Tendons and flesh appear. Still there is no life. Then the Lord says, "Come from the four winds, O breath, and breathe into these slain." The bodies come to life and stand on their feet as a vast army.[5]

Jesus alive. He walks into the room where his fearful disciples are cowering in the shadows. "As the Father hath sent me, I am sending you." With this, Jesus breathes on them and says, "Receive the Holy Spirit. If you forgive anyone his sins, they are forgiven; if you do not forgive them, they are not forgiven."[6]

I awake to find myself in the hospital chair. For the first time, I notice the crucifix on the wall. Jesus is struggling to

3 Genesis 2:7.
4 1 Kings 17:17–24.
5 Ezekiel 37:12, 14.
6 John 20:21–23.

breathe. Unable to support his weight, he tries to open up his lungs as gravity forces his chest cavity down. He manages only six short sentences, then says, "It is finished." He gives up his last breath so that we can come alive by the breath of the Spirit.

I look at my brother-in-law on his hospital bed. He is still breathing. Where there is breath, there is Spirit. Where there is Spirit, there is life and hope. "Let everything that hath breath praise the Lord."

Breathe in. Breathe out.

My brother-in-law William Jess Mitchell not only survived his illness but lived through a tornado that touched down near the hospital. He was airlifted to his home in Knoxville, Tennessee, where he spent another month in the hospital. He lived five more productive and happy years enjoying his family. They called him Mr. M&M, the miracle man.

Beauty Leads to God

All beauty leads us to God.

—Abbot Suger

I am helping my seventh-grade grandson, Pete, work on an essay about a saying from Abbot Suger, a twelfth-century French abbot and statesman. I am trying to talk about the quote, but Pete does not want to think about it. He is discouraged.

His study room is not yet set up; the walls are the color of sand, but there are no pictures or artwork. "What do you think?" I said, trying again. "Does beauty lead us to God? Or away from God?"

"Beauty is in the eye of the one who sees it," he says. I am impressed. We're getting somewhere. "Some bands play music that leads you to God. The same kind of music in the hands of another group leads to drinking, taking drugs, running from the law."

He's satisfied that he's said enough. He doesn't understand why I want him to elaborate and make it look like a paper. However, when a child hits an adult with some simple wisdom, it can hit hard. "Beauty is in the eye of the one who sees it." I can't get it out of my mind.

I have not given beauty much thought. In fact, beauty has been the last thing on my mind. Neatness, orderliness, decency —these are important. But beauty? I tell Pete about the woman in the Bible who poured a costly bottle of nard over the feet of Jesus. Others protest the extravagance; Jesus says she has done a beautiful thing for him.

I think of all the places I have tried to study or read and how little conscious attention I paid to the external beauty in my surroundings. While I was a pastor in Brazil, a friend let me use his empty apartment to prepare a sermon. The walls were painted but blank. It didn't matter. My face was in my lexicon and commentary and dictionary. But I remember that I was drawn to the curtainless window. Here, through clear glass, I could see the sun lighting up the bright Portuguese tiles on the buildings and, behind them, the light on the tops of the trees.

While Pete and I debate whether he has written enough, his screensaver comes on and runs through color closeups of a brilliant yellow flower, a hummingbird, some multicolored leaves, a grain of salt, and his baby sister. He shows me that while I was fretting about his homework assignment, he has made a design of three wires—copper, tin, and steel—by bending them into a closed rectangle. "These are three different metals, connected to work together," he explains. Pete has gotten the message: beauty and the simplicity of a child leads to God.

Now back in my own home, I look at the arrangements of magnolia and decorative grasses that a friend from Brazil has made. I see the delicate leaves and their shades of green. I notice how the yellow glow of a chandelier lamp warms the colors of a painting on the wall. Then I turn to my devotional reading for the day. It's about Jesus and his transfiguration. In front of his closest friends, his face becomes full of glory and his clothes dazzling white. Beauty leads to God.

Come-unto-Me Church

I had visited Atlanta's Pine Street Shelter for the homeless a decade earlier, but it was a quick in-and-out with college students on an Atlanta urban tour. This Sunday afternoon is different. I am the preacher. I have been arm-twisted into this by two of our church members who don't know the meaning of "no," especially when it comes to helping people on the margins. They believe that God has called my church, North Avenue Presbyterian, to offer worship services and food to homeless men. They also believe I am supposed to be one of the regular preachers, if not *the* preacher.

The shelter is an old garage and auto dealership, built in the 1930s. As Alexandra and I walk to the entrance, we pass poorly dressed men lining the sidewalk. They stop talking and eye us warily. We walk up an old concrete car ramp next to a permanently closed garage door and into a massive concrete room where mechanics used to work on broken-down vehicles.

The cavernous room is lit by four mercury vapor streetlights hanging from a high ceiling. Their incandescent light makes the room feel like an impersonal bus station where people gather on their road to somewhere else. But there are over four hundred men here, some sitting, some sleeping, waiting to go nowhere. Two fans on wobbly poles do little to move the increasingly stale air.

"This is one of the funniest things I've ever seen," I tell Alexandra. "They are expecting me to preach, but there is no PA system. In this huge room, I can't even see everyone, much less make myself heard."

My partner is a singer who plays an electric guitar with a backup band. She's accustomed to lots of mikes and computer-driven overheads. This afternoon she is just a little girl with a tiny guitar. I look at her and lift my eyebrows with a silent question—*What are you going to do?* She shrugs. I think, *Oh God, if anything is going to happen here today, it is up to you.*

"Sing as long as you can," I tell the woman, "because I have no idea what I am going to say." I mentally cut my sermon in half, and then cut and cut it again. I try to reduce my complicated message to a single point. I tell myself that the gospel stories come from an oral and verbal tradition rather than from manuscripts or overhead projectors. I think of Peter preaching at Pentecost. No notes. No preparation. He quotes David, "I saw the Lord always before me that I should not be shaken."[7] Three thousand people respond with belief.

"Wherever you are, whatever you do or have done, God is there too," I say with a loud voice, adding a few paragraphs of elaboration. The men listen politely, grateful for a short sermon. Then they quickly line up for the sack lunches prepared by some of our Sunday school classes. The line becomes a moving circle around the perimeter of the room as the men loop back for more food. We run out of lunches somewhere in the second loop.

A man comes up to me to ask what church we come from. I tell him. He doesn't recognize the name. I describe its color. Gray stone, like Stone Mountain. The light comes on in his eyes. "Oh, you mean the come-unto-me church." I think he is confused. I explain again the location and color. He repeats, "The come-unto-me church."

7 Acts 2:17.

I remember that on the church wall that faces north there is a tiled icon of Jesus. His eyes are the all-knowing Byzantine type, and his pierced hands are extended outward in a welcoming gesture. Beneath his feet are these words: "Come unto me all you that are weary and heavy laden, and I will give you rest." As a pedestrian, the man in the shelter might see it every day, but if you are driving in from the suburbs, you may never see it.

"That's right," I say, "The come-unto-me church." He nods and smiles. I have come today to help some men down on their luck spend some time with Jesus. But just for this moment, through this homeless man, Jesus has come to be with me.

I Have Been to the Mountaintop

It is four o'clock on a cool Saturday afternoon in the North Georgia mountains. I am attending an annual men's retreat at a camp usually reserved for teenagers. The camp sits in a valley between two fast-moving streams. One flows toward Mount Oglethorpe, which was the southern terminus of the Appalachian Trail before its pristine wilderness was marred by roads and chicken farms. The other stream flows toward Sharp Top Mountain, a distinctive cone-shaped peak rising out of the foothills of Pickens County, near the county seat of Jasper, Georgia.

I am standing on a gravel road at the base of Sharp Top, looking around for someone who is willing to climb with me. They will need to be a patient person, as I have never made it more than two hundred yards from the trailhead, where the grade abruptly changes from medium gradual to acute. My usual hiking companion, a man from Cullman, Alabama, was not able to come to camp this year. He owns an outdoor store and has sent me some new hiking poles. I know it is unlikely that I will find a fellow hiker as accommodating as he is.

Almost fifteen years earlier I had been diagnosed with claudication—pain in the legs upon exercising that is caused by an inadequate blood flow to my leg muscles. It is like having a clogged fuel line in your car. If you stop and rest and let the blood flow catch up, you can walk through the pain.

I have recently undergone a medical procedure to correct the blood flow in my legs, and I am eager to try out my new legs. I am about to begin walking on my own when two young men in their twenties appear. They are looking for the trail to Sharp Top. I offer to take them as far as the trailhead, which is about a mile away on gravel road. We walk together, and I tire quickly. I can see that I am no match for them.

I point to the trailhead. "From here it goes up steadily at a twenty percent grade or more and then gets steeper at the summit. I am too tired. You go on."

Their young legs carry them up the trail, and they disappear around a bend. I stand, rest, and drink some water. In four or five minutes I check in with my legs. "Let's just try going up a little ways," I suggest. So we climb a few minutes. It's steep. We rest. "Can we try again?" I ask my legs.

I hear talking ahead. A group of young men has stopped along the way. I try to reach them, but by the time I get there, they have moved on. I am alone. I keep walking. I see an ancient Appalachian peak covered with color, and I think I am close to the end. It is a false summit.

"I won't even think about the next summit," I assure my legs. "We'll just go to the next switchback and stop and see how we're doing." Life is more than mountaintops, my right brain suggests. Let's enjoy the climb.

I hear voices. Two dogs, then children stop and stare at me. I put on my most nonmenacing smile. The children are silent, waiting for their mothers, who arrive right behind them.

"How was the climb?" That is nonthreatening enough.

"Oh, it's tough. But the dogs made it. And the kids."

Next come the husbands, late boomers limping with their football knees clearly in distress. They confirm that the remaining climb is tough, very tough. How far? "Maybe you've come halfway."

Maybe halfway? I wish I hadn't heard them. I have to enjoy this climb, because a summit is out of the question. "Let's go until five o'clock and see where we are." My body agrees. We walk a bit more.

Remember that group of guys ahead of me that I was not able to catch up with? Here they come back down. How was the climb? "Steep. We couldn't see the top. We're going back." That's discouraging. "Let's keep on a little bit longer," I tell myself. I promise to turn around. Just five more minutes. Then another five.

I hear voices. It's the two young men I guided to the trailhead coming back down.

"Tom, look at you!"

"Yeah, it's me, the tortoise."

"You are almost at the top," they say. "Come on, we'll go with you." They assure me that they don't mind my slow pace. I tell them that I am not going to look ahead. "I don't want the climb to freak me out. I am going to depend on you to guide me."

"We will guide you all the way."

My legs are tired, but the wind is picking up, and the thought of summiting gives my legs a little adrenaline to run on.

"We are here, Tom. Look up!"

Wind and lightning have cleared away the big trees from the granite summit. I can see for 360 degrees. There is Jasper and Grandview Lake, and then the highway that pulls out of Talking Rock and climbs the next mountain.

I thank my guides many times over and pick up a few rocks. Will anyone believe?

I think of Martin Luther King Jr. on his last night on earth. "I have been to the mountaintop." He had met God, been transfigured, and seen the Promised Land. Some people believe he knew that night he wasn't going to live long enough to see the descendants of slaves and of free white people live together in true reconciliation. But he believed.

Now I believe too. I have reached the summit by enjoying the climb one step at a time. I was given personal guides—a guide is always better than a map—and I had cheerleaders. I have found a way to transcend my physical and emotional disabilities to find contentment in being a wisdom figure rather than a vigorous outdoorsman. I am learning to make mortality a friend, not a dreaded enemy. And yet I am reconnecting with my youth and the young of a new generation.

The view for now is good. I cannot see tomorrow, and I don't know how much farther these legs will take me or what rivers and valleys we will cross. But I have been to the mountaintop, and that is enough for today.

Socks

I love warm socks in the winter—more than hats, scarves, or gloves. Give me some thick woolen socks. Then I can brave the cold, the wind, and the freezing rain. Warm feet, warm body.

I like to find woolen socks on sale in the spring. Put them up for the summer. Then when it is really cold, I pull them out, slip on some water-resistant shoes and go out into the cold. What could feel better?

Ask a foot soldier what he values most in the winter, and he will probably say warm, dry, clean socks. A homeless person the same. Ever see a homeless woman in the winter in hose? No, only in socks.

Since socks tend to disappear in the washing machine and dryer, I wash them by hand. I have had several pairs that went into the dryer and came out as children's socks. No thank you, I'll wash my own.

Nursing home directors say that the biggest single complaint from residents and their families is socks. Lost, "stolen" socks. My aunt Lib, who has gone on to be with Jesus, wouldn't let anyone buy her socks except my brother Pat. She didn't trust anyone else. Her socks came in six-packs; she wanted just three.

"Take the rest back, Pat."

"I can't take them back, Lib."

"Well, you can't leave them here. Someone will steal them."

You think I am neurotic? I saw a diagram of the feet created by a Korean reflexologist. One part of the foot controls the large intestine, another the small intestine, another the pancreas. He was saying what I knew all along. Keep your intestines and pancreas warm by covering your feet.

✦ ☙ ✦

I am in the ICU with Alexandra, checking the monitor and watching our friend Bill Carlson struggle to breathe. The oxygen uptake is too low. As we turn to leave, Alexandra asks me to check his feet. They are like ice.

I ask his wife, "Betty, does he have any socks?"

"No."

Only one thing to do—take off my new wool socks and put them on Bill. No matter that I look funny walking down the corridor with no socks. Late that afternoon, Bill slips away, but he goes with warm feet.

If Jesus was here among us this winter and said, "When I was sick you visited me," he might add, "And you brought me a pair of warm socks." This Christmas I am going to carry a bag of socks in my car. If a homeless person asks for money, I may or may not give it to him, but I will surprise him with a pair of socks.

Try it yourself. This Christmas, don't just fill stockings. Give socks.

By the way, Bill Carlson didn't leave my socks. They just disappeared. If you run into an angel with black socks and he answers to "Bill," ask him to bring me back my socks.

Betty and Bill Carlson were our longtime neighbors and friends. Bill was a practical joker. One evening at the home of a prominent Atlanta couple, Bill planted silverware in my suit pocket and told the hostess that I had a problem with collecting other people's silver. We helped start a Prison Fellowship group at the Atlanta penitentiary, and on a visit, I lured him into a cell and closed the door. But in the end, Bill won. He got my new wool socks.

A Christmas P-Mail

Alexandra and I are both sick. And it is Christmastime. We are convinced that we have picked up some exotic virus in Brazil until we learn that everyone in Atlanta seems to be catching the same bug.

I have so much to do. From my bed, I send e-mails. Suddenly there's a glitch—my computer's screen display shrinks in size. No problem. I find stronger reading glasses. Then my server abruptly shuts down completely. Not to worry. I drag myself out of bed and go to the office. The server crashes just as I arrive—all data lost. I go home to use the phone. My voice cuts out.

Now I am really shut off from the outside world. I give up; I am out of ideas. I take to bed, in a fetal position. While I'm lying there, I get an inspiration. A phrase from the Bible runs through my head:

> Their voice goes out into all the earth,
> their words to the ends of the world.[8]

It's just the beginning of the verses that come to me with a force as if they had been spoken out loud.

> So is my word that goes out from my mouth:
> It will not return to me empty.[9]

I wonder—What does it all mean? Can I log on to the Lord's network and send out a message? Nothing else is working, so why not give it a try? People and places flash through my mind.

8 Psalm 19:4 (NIV).
9 Isaiah 55:11 (NIV).

I send messages of blessing at the speed of light to friends and families, some living in comfortable homes and some living on the streets of Brazil, Jamaica, and Atlanta. I pick up steam and move on to Africa and Asia and even places I have never been before.

I don't know if my messages get through, but when I hit the Send button, they don't bounce back. I feel connected. I call it prayer mail or p-mail.

My mind wanders to a friend who is sick. "I am too tired to pray," he had told me on a recent visit to his bedside.

"Then send your thoughts," I had suggested. "Do you have strength for that?"

He said that he did. I told him his thoughts were merely prevocalized prayers.

Now I am following my own advice. I think of a friend who lives in Florida who has developed a cancerous node on a vocal cord. Doctors cut out the node, and he has begun radiation. Every day his whisper has grown fainter, until now he cannot make a sound. He has always been a great communicator, and I know the forced silence is taking a toll. I lie in bed and send him p-mails. (Several months later he will call me, still speaking in a whisper. It seems as if we had never been out of touch.)

Still lying in bed, my thoughts turn back decades. I am sixteen and very discouraged. At boarding school I attend a meeting and hear for the first time—although it has been said many times before—that God loves me. I call my mother a few nights later and tell her about my experience.

"Which evening?" she asks.

"Sunday."

"On that very night I sent you a message that God loves you," she told me. "God sent me back a message—*peace*."

Dear reader, I send you a p-mail message—of shalom, peace, blessing, and companionship. It is faster than e-mail.

Shack Living

Out of the house with the dog for a late-night walk to clear my mind. Feeling troubled, tired, confused—by what I cannot remember.

Over a neighbor's roof I see Orion rising off his back to face the Bull. Orion's belt is three stars perpendicular to the horizon, and in my mind I take a ride to visit them. They are magnificent. *One day I will visit there.* This thought lets me break through the heavy, dark roof that seems to confine me.

Standing under the stars, I am reminded of a book I have just read that described the constricting nature of human experience. We live alone in a shack, the authors reflected, with the windows shuttered and only narrow lines of light showing through.

> The furnishings never change because we feel secure
> only if we are familiar with everything in our room....
> When the latches come off and the door is opened—
> when we walk out into a world filled with light and
> life—we will be disoriented. We may even shuffle back
> into the room and close the door, leaving it cracked
> only a little, in order to summon up courage to go
> back out.[10]

I see myself as a child, lying on a bed in my room that faces a bend in the road. It is dark, but as a car comes and goes, my room is swept by a light from outside. Someday, I tell myself,

10 Tom and Patrick Malone, *Windows of Experience* (New York: Simon & Schuster, 1992).

I will break free from the four walls that define the parameters of my life.

I take one last look at the stars and reluctantly head home. I walk through the door, and it is there, under my own roof and shut off from the stars, that I see the light in the eyes of my wife. Thanks to the laser beams of distant stars, I can see the spark of life in someone right in front of me. *The Word became flesh and made his dwelling among us.*

Perhaps, I think to myself, it was something like this for the shepherds keeping watch over their flocks by night. The angels appear. The sky is filled with light. The music of angelic voices cascades off the Galilean hills. Just as suddenly everything becomes quiet. The shepherds make the dark trip down the mountain to a stable, following as best they can the light they have been given. Then they see it: the light in the mother's eyes and the light falling on the peaceful sleeping child. The Light comes to the shack in Bethlehem.

❖ ☗ ❖

I was still thinking about light and shacks the next morning, when I stopped by the office where I had worked for over ten years. Our organization and other nonprofits had shared so much history in the building. It was like a worn-out shoe— creaky, cranky, cold, comfortable.

The church that owned the building was about to demolish it as part of a redevelopment plan. The building needed to go. It was a pre-Depression shack, and not many improvements had been made since it was built. But it was our shack, our home. Our family of ministries had grown up there together and then, one by one, moved away. My organization was going to be the last to leave.

The wind rushed through the empty hall. I looked at the ceiling tiles that had soaked up so much rain. We had felt a certain pride in our shack. We held it all together with tape and plastic and pitch and showed how cheaply a nonprofit can live. But there was a downside. The boarded-up windows kept out the light and limited our vision.

Now I have taken a ride to another galaxy, I thought to myself. I am ready to move out of my shack.

I am the world's light. No one who follows me stumbles around in the darkness, I provide plenty of light to live in.[11] The person who said this must have lived in a few shacks.

11 John 8:12 (The Message).

WINTER

Making It Through January

Before I start making Herculean plans for a new year, I try to make it through January.

Here's what is good about January. I enjoy bundling up and walking in the cold. I marvel at bare trees showing off their intricate infrastructure. In Atlanta, jonquils and crocuses send up their green spears like periscopes, peeking through the brown and black remains of autumn to check out the cold landscape of winter. On clear nights, Orion chases the Bull across the frosty sky.

But January has a harsh side. Some of my worst illnesses —flu and pneumonia—have been in January. My mother, my mother-in-law, and my brother-in-law all became ill and died in January. While skiing in January, my good friend and colleague in ministry Jerry Franz had a heart attack and died a week later. My pastor and colleague Frank Harrington died of an illness that began in January.

I do not have happy memories of hospitals and cemeteries in January. This does not mean that I am a pessimist, but I have enough memories filed away to be careful. I have learned that January is not the month for launching major offensives. We should treat it like adolescence—just try to make it through without any major catastrophes.

My mother understood this. She let us play in the snow but not stay in it. Before our wet mittens became cakes of ice, she rang a bell. She called us into the garage and sent us down the basement stairs into a room dominated by a coal-burning furnace. Here we dropped our wet clothing in a frosty puddle and put on dry and warmed woolens. Then we sat at her table, drinking hot chocolate and telling stories about our daring rides—sledding double down the steep hill in front of the house or dodging dogwoods on the back hill.

Some say, "But this is Atlanta, and the sun is shining!" Caution is needed. It is not yet spring. Watch the trees. They are quietly gathering strength, waiting. Their buds are hard and coated. They are holding back, alert for the signal to burst forth. With luck, the warm snap will not continue. If it does, their tender buds will open prematurely only to be burned black by the cold. They will not make it through January.

January is a time of preparation, a time to take in, to strengthen roots, to hibernate, to cogitate, to huddle, to watch the colorful dance of fire. "Bring my cloak and my scrolls, especially the parchment," the apostle Paul wrote to his young friend Timothy. "Do your best to come before winter."[12]

January is wrap-yourself-in-a-blanket season, a time to settle in with a good book or pen and paper in front of a fire. A time to meditate and pray and read sacred Scripture. It is also a time to give a caring ear to the vulnerable. Winter thins out the herd. Some who appear to be hibernating are in fact dying. The depressed don't call to make appointments. Maybe we should not fill our schedules with everyone who wants to see us with some new idea, but we should save some time to check on those who don't call.

Perhaps my concern is just another exaggerated fear like the Y2K scare at the end of the millennium. Perhaps the flu epidemic is just drug-company hype. Maybe we will lick pneumonia.

12 2 Timothy 4:13, 21.

Maybe there will be enough sunshine to bake us out of despondency and depression. Spring will come early, and we will pack away the woolens the second week of February.

But just in case, I am going to feed the roots and not send the young shoots out too soon. I don't want them to be burned black by a late, killing freeze. I'll stay bundled up a few more weeks, savoring the cold. I won't rush spring.

My Neighbor Jabez

Dear Jabez,

You are making a big hit. Have we ever witnessed this in modern times—a comeback after some three thousand years of silence from a person as little known as you? You are much bigger now than when you were alive.

Your current fame is based on a prayer that was recorded in the sacred history of Israel. You called on God, and God granted your request:

> Oh, that you would bless me indeed and enlarge my
> territory, that Your hand would be with me, and that
> You would keep me from evil, that I may not cause
> pain.[13]

This prayer has made it to the big time because of an author, Bruce Wilkinson, who has been talking you up for years. He published a book, *The Prayer of Jabez,* which has sold eleven million copies. My own secretary bought the book in bulk and gave it away to friends and strangers. One Christmas I received three copies as gifts. Each one was inscribed by a friend, so I couldn't figure out how to give the extras away. Instead, I read from one, then another.

I do not know if this is what you had in mind, Mr. Jabez, when you created your prayer. I admit I say it quite often: "Oh, Lord, bless me and enlarge my territory." And God has done just this. I heard a preacher shout this message, and my life was

13 1 Chronicles 4:9–10.

transformed. I came into the arena a wounded lamb and went out a roaring lion. "I am not going to let those people push me around anymore."

And my wife, too—you should hear her. Instead of asking permission for how much air she can breathe for fear of taking oxygen from someone else, she is on the phone encouraging people up a storm. She is in her car, taking food and comfort to people who need it. She invites people into our home.

So thank you, Jabez. Thank you, scribes of Israel, for including this prayer in your records. Thank you, present-day scribe Bruce Wilkinson. Too many of us have held back from what we felt God calling us to do because we lacked courage and resources. "Oh, that you would bless me indeed and enlarge my territory, that Your hand would be with me!"

Now, Jabez, since I am asking God to bless me and increase my borders, my territory, my whatever, and since I am trying not to be mealymouthed, overly timid, or weak-kneed anymore, would you mind if I point out some abuses of your prayer?

Enlarge my territory. I was just in Jamaica, and the only Christian television I could find were ranting white and black preachers from the United States with their big-hair blondes and big-signal stations. There were a few local pastors and evange-lists speaking the language of their people, but their budgets and signals were weak. Christian radio announcers from the United States brag that they broadcast to an ever-increasing number of countries. And there are churches that want to send short-term missionaries for two days or two weeks to every continent of the world.

Jabez, your prayer is being used to appeal to our fallen nature, to our desire to control and to rule. Rather than lifting up the names of Yahweh and Jesus, we want to stamp our own brand name on every tribe and every nation.

That you would keep me from evil, that I may not cause pain. Our effort to enlarge our territory, to substitute the name of our organization for Jesus, is the same evil lived out by the people of Babel who wanted to dominate the earth. Jabez, do you know how much pain those of us in the modern world cause when we go in with our big budgets and big programs and our American faces and conquering mentality and set up our tent on top of an indigenous work? Do you know the pain we cause when we do not even take the time to find partners, to strengthen struggling works, to help our neighbors enlarge and strengthen their own territory? Save us from those who pray only half the prayer.

Jabez, I am only able to write you because you have encouraged me to increase my territory. I hope this is not painful but helpful.

Sincerely and forcefully,

Your neighbor,

Tom Roddy

Cold Feet

Cold feet. I was born with them. Fortunately my mother taught me about wool socks, galoshes, and shoes that don't leak—full neolyte soles and sealer around the seams. Even so, I've been a little cautious. I've been careful to learn everything I can before I plunge in. I remind myself that, if I have to jump, I need to go feet first. Never dive.

I get cold feet before stressful moments. Like several years ago, when I was being wheeled into the operating room for a hernia repair. It's not pleasant. They shave all the hair off, dress you in a nightgown open at the back, and cover you with a thin sheet. Maybe they think your chances of survival are better if your body is just above freezing.

"Do you have any questions?" the anesthesiologist asked.

"Yes. Would you mind covering my feet?"

I think of my friend Ben Picone, who played for the Atlanta Symphony. He survived several strokes but eventually passed beyond medical hope for recovery. When he went off life support, his wife and son and everyone else told him good-bye. Then he lingered another three months.

The last time I visited him, he talked to me in monosyllables. I noticed his feet were uncovered. Being curious about feet, I touched them. Cold as ice.

"Your feet are cold."

"Yeah."

I found his socks and put them on his feet.

"Is that all right?"

"Yeah."

My father suffered a bad fall in 1993 on the weekend that a storm of the century hit much of the country. The snow closed roads and held doctors and nurses hostage wherever they were. I was able to get from Atlanta to the hospital in Knoxville, but the medical crew had not been home for days.

When I touched my father's feet in his chilly hospital room, they were as cold as ice. I took off my snow boots and put my wool hiking socks on his feet. It seemed the least I could do. Now I would have to walk back to the motel, through a foot and half of snow, without socks. (By now, you are realizing that giving away socks in the hospital is a pattern for me.)

A nurse breezed in and saw the heavy wool socks. They were obviously not hospital booties. "Who did this?" she demanded, glaring at me. She made it sound like I had pulled out his IV.

"I did. Feel my hands, my feet," I said. "Are they cold? My feet and his—they are just the same."

The nurse walked out, and the socks stayed on. I felt triumphant. Thanks to me, when my father approached Jordan's stormy banks at least his feet would be warm.

At their funerals, both Ben and my father marched out to *Ein Feste Burg*. I like to think that having warm feet helped them get where they were going.

> A mighty fortress is our God, a bulwark never failing;
> A helper he amid the flood
> Of mortal ills prevailing.

As I write this, I'm getting ready to return to Brazil to be with friends who are walking in hard places. They are congressional leaders and presidential aides, health workers battling against AIDS, and community organizers fighting for the rights of *os abandonados*—the abandoned children. My feet are getting a little cold, and it's not just pre-travel jitters. I am afraid that my firsthand encounter with such intense suffering will be too much to handle.

My friends working in urban communities in the United States are getting cold feet too. They are facing increasing violence, gang warfare, and hopeless poverty. For all of us, the stressors accumulate—health, finances, school, jobs, relationships. The world is changing, and nothing is the same, nor can it be. Our feet are getting cold.

Over the years, I've learned a cure for cold feet. Walk or run on them. With or without socks. Take with you the good news of liberation—the blind see, the lame walk, the lepers are cleansed, the deaf hear. The dead are raised and the poor hear good news.

"How beautiful upon the mountains are the feet of him who brings good tidings, who publishes peace."[14]

I know many brave people with cold feet.

---

14 Isaiah 52:7.

Presence of the Poor

I am in Washington, DC, to attend the National Prayer Breakfast. Alexandra and I have just finished eating with friends at an upscale restaurant in the trendy Adams Morgan neighborhood. It is Havana night, and we are full of romantic Latin tunes and savory Cuban food. We walk out the door into a frigid wintry evening where, counting the wind chill, the temperature is five below.

A person is standing on the sidewalk, holding out a Styrofoam cup and begging for spare change. I don't even know if it is a man or a woman. He or she is wearing a formless army jacket, and all that is visible beneath the navy beanie is a pair of dark piercing eyes.

I quickly brush past the cup and instruct the rest of our party to do the same. My wife, Alexandra, is having none of it. She greets the mystery person as if he or she is a long-lost friend and discovers that her name is Ayisha. They are soon arm in arm, and we are off to buy Ayisha supper.

"Whatever she wants, I am treating," says Alexandra.

I am furious. We have our guests. The street is dangerous. Although it was twenty-five years ago, I still vividly remember being robbed at gunpoint just two blocks away. But I cannot leave my wife, and I know that she is right.

I remember the prophetic words of a West Indian ambassador as he spoke to our group of people from the Caribbean at the National Prayer Breakfast. "It is good to eat well and be in fellowship with important people, as we are today," he said. "But what will we do if a homeless person walks through that door and wants to be part of our circle?"

I lamely wave good-bye to my friends and follow my wife and Ayisha into a fast-food Chinese restaurant. The proprietor is as surprised as I am. In an all-out-effort to get rid of us, he turns the heat off and shoots the air conditioner up full blast.

"We are paying customers," Ayisha yells at the manager. "You are not going to get rid of us!"

Halfway through her meal, Ayisha looks up from her food. "What is the matter?" she asks me. "Why are you sad?"

"Well, for starters, I had to leave my guests on the street."

She looks at me with a slight smile. "You should not be sad," she says. "You got to have dinner with your friends, and now you get to have dinner with me."

Her words gave me a new take on the puzzling words of Jesus. "The poor you will always have with you."[15] Another homeless person once told me, "The poor you will always *get* to have with you." He was right, and so was Ayisha. I was privileged, reluctantly, to share a meal with her. She was a present—a gift from God.

Ayisha buttoned up her army coat, put on her navy beanie, and headed for the door. As she stepped outside, she gave a sneer in the direction of the manager and held the door open a few moments longer than necessary to let the cold air rush in.

I never saw her again, but a month later I told this story to singer and songwriter Ken Medema during a mission conference at my church in downtown Atlanta. Ken, who is blind, sang an impromptu song that ended with these words:

15 Matthew 26:11.

But don't you understand, Sir Tom, and don't you
plainly see? I am the face of Jesus Christ, and you have
dined with me.

The poor we get to have with us.

And she might have been the woman at the Pharisee's banquet
who knelt by Jesus' feet.
Ayisha might well have been her name. This woman, o' so
sweet.
"Who is this tramp who comes in here? We do not need her
kind."
But the Kingdom of God is for fools like this. Now, that truth
can change your mind.

Now lived a restaurant owner just like that when Jesus came
to eat.
"Who is this woman, this woman from the streets, who comes
to anoint your feet?
She wipes your feet with her long, long hair, and I just don't
understand."
The Kingdom of God is for fools like this. You see it is a fool's
play land.

Now you need not fret, brother Tom. You need not have a care.
You left your friends behind you, across the street over there.

But don't you understand, Sir Tom, and don't you plainly see?
I am the face of Jesus Christ, and you have dined with me.

©Ken Medema, February 1995

Dread

It was midwinter, and I was full of dread. The day had finally come to move my nonprofit organization out of the old theater building that had been our home for many years. The building was about to be torn down, and another nonprofit—Urban Young Life for teenagers—was going with me. We were the last survivors of our urban encampment that in its heyday included five nonprofits. We had all been roughing it, in the heart of an Atlanta high-rent district, in an affordable but rundown office space.

I dreaded moving. Going through my own memories and the trash of other people was a bit like death—except when I died, someone else would be doing the sorting. So I was in pain. The new office would be a great deal smaller, and I had to leave behind a lot of old friends, including the steel desk used by my father's secretary. I had recycled it three or four times now, but now it had to go.

I met him when I was unloading the trash from my fifteen-foot Ryder truck. He was standing by the Dumpster behind the office. "Let me help you," he said. "I keep this place clean." He had a friendly smile and neatly trimmed dreadlocks. I didn't really need help, and I didn't want him going through my papers. But, then, everyone can use a friend at the Dumpster.

"Yeah, sure, give me a hand," I said a bit grudgingly. "I am Tom."

"I am Dread, as in dreadlocks." He looked over the cans of paint in the truck bed. "You let that paint freeze. Read the label. It's no good now. I'll throw it out for you."

"I'm good in construction," he added matter-of-factly. "You see that house? I built it." He pointed to a small hut constructed from scrap lumber, plastic, old doors, and rugs.

"The church lets me live here. I take care of the place."

When we finished cleaning out the truck bed, Dread guided me with hand signals while I backed the truck up to a narrow, kudzu-covered ramp that led to the backdoor and an elevator. I remembered the words of the Ryder agent: "Don't scratch it; it's brand-new."

Teenagers from urban and suburban Young Life clubs spilled out of the building and down the ramps like ants, bringing the furniture and boxes to be moved to our new location. Dread directed the operation and carefully packed the truck so that the load was secure and well balanced. When we were finished, we paid him and thanked him.

From the pile of stuff we left behind, Dread asked only for a stuffed raccoon and a stuffed vulture (they had been white elephant gifts), and an old *Atlanta Journal* from around 1945. It was fine with me. Only later did I wonder what a homeless man would want with an old newspaper and some stuffed animals.

"I won't let nobody mess up this place back here or get into that door," Dread promised. "Come see me when you come back."

When I last saw Dread, he was wheeling a shopping cart down Peachtree Street, gathering other people's junk and selling it. I admired his creative entrepreneurship and remembered how he had turned a dreaded move into an almost joyful experience. His plastic-sided shack was gone, torn down along with the theater. But I was sure that he had found other people to be with, to help out and to bless. Because the poor you always get to have with you.

Tucking In Mom

Hush little baby now don't you cry cause your mother
is gone
When she's gone on home, when mother is gone
Hush little baby now don't you cry
You'll see your mother in the by and by
Motherless children have a hard time when the mother
is gone
When she's gone on home when your mother is gone

—"Motherless Children"
(traditional, arrangement by Tim O'Brien)[16]

Knoxville, Tennessee, January 1981. My mother is in the hospital, and I am visiting her after Sunday church. The reality that she is dying is hard to face. Strange that this is the same hospital where she brought me into the world.

I head back to my parents' home to check on my father and go for a run through the hills of my grandfather's old farm in Knox County, Tennessee. My dad's father, whom I called Pop Pops, nursed this Depression land back from death with the help of a caretaker. They filled in eroded gullies and rotated cattle and crops to nourish the soil. Since childhood, it is the place where I have gone to clear my mind.

I begin my run in an old-growth woods that my grandfather never permitted to be logged. As an imaginative boy, I had seen it as an enchanted forest. I had spent days here searching for

16 From *Remember Me,* Howdy Skies Music, ASCAP.

animal footprints or dashing through the gloom until I saw sunlight streaming through the branches ahead of me. Now I find myself running again toward the light at the edge of the woods.

I head down a grassy glen toward the creek and follow the tree line toward a barn made from old Coca-Cola signs. As children we had fought World War II skirmishes here in the haylofts. We guided newcomers to gaps in the floor covered by new hay, and with just the right step, the unsuspecting victim disappeared into the pile of old hay below. Today, as I come up the hill, I am shocked to find the barn burned to the ground. I knew that the two barns and the oldest house on the property had been torched by vandals in the fall, but I was not expecting ashes.

I keep running, heading up a row of walnut trees toward the old kite barn. My maternal grandfather was an inventive lawyer, and he had experimented with flight in this barn. It was a makeshift hangar for his giant white kites that were taller than a man and wider than his reach. Now all that remains are a few charred boards.

I move on to a road that is just faint indentations in overgrown grass. A few years earlier, it had been two parallel tire tracks covered with gravel. I come to the remains of the farmhouse where I spent my first year of life. The old house, as we called it, was full of secret passages under its eaves, and it groaned and rattled in the wind. As kids we pretended to be grown-ups here, telling ghost stories while someone played scary notes on an old pump organ. Now this farmhouse, too, is ashes and blackened boards.

I run into the old orchard where Pop Pops took me to taste his muscadine grapes and tangy apples. Without my grandfather's constant care, the grapevines have all but disappeared.

The apple trees have become wild and woody and twice their normal size. Except for a few hard, acorn-sized fruits, they have lost their fruit-bearing capacity.

There is no running away from it now: the dream farm of Pop Pops is in shambles. Perhaps we could have turned the homeplace into a showcase, something that would have made him proud, but here it is—ashes and overgrown orchards.

Through the bare winter branches of a stand of walnut trees, I look out on my parents' home. It is a redbrick Colonial house with white columns and a tiled verandah. How many games of football, softball, and cowboys and Indians had I played on its sloping lawn? Like the giant oak trees around it, which have survived years of drought, it still seems ageless.

My father is in the kitchen, which he has converted to his study, den, and office. He is sitting in his favorite chair in a faded woolen shirt, watching old movies. He is alone. Mother is not here, and she is never coming back. What will happen to their home? Will it one day be in shambles too?

I feel my hope dwindling. I have stumbled upon my roots and found decay. Mother's tired body doing its best to keep going. Dad carrying on seemingly without much to live for. Pop Pops' body in the ground, his dream gone.

I turn and look to the south. Before me is the Rocky Hill Baptist Church, its steeple lit by the setting sun. Quite suddenly the word of the Lord comes to me:

Why do you seek the living among the dead? He is not here; he is risen. Pop Pops is not here. Soon your mother will not be here either.

Your hope is not in what remains, in trying to keep

alive an old barn or to preserve a farm within a city.
Don't seek your new life among the blackened ruins.
Your hope is in the resurrection of the dead.

I run the rest of the way home. I sit with Dad in front of the television and watch Dallas beat Atlanta in the NFL playoffs. I shower and drive to the hospital. I tell my mother stories. I hold her hand and tell her that soon a strong hand will reach out for her. *Put your hand in his.* Before I leave, we say a goodnight prayer together, and I tuck her in. I wave at the nurses as I walk by their station. They have tears in their eyes; they have heard every word I said.

In less than ten hours Mom fades into a coma, and two days later, she slips from death into life.

Where There Is Hope, There Is Help

Where there is hope, there is help. Think about it. When we have no hope, there is no strength to help ourselves or others. We rarely give where the need is the greatest but where hope is the greatest. It is easier to give scholarships to poor kids trying to go to college than to a homeless person on the street asking for money. How much help fledgling democracies receive from the United States, at least in theory, ultimately rests on how much hope we have that their democracies will survive. Where there is hope, there is help.

Near our mountain home in East Tennessee, Appalachian old-timers ask, "May I hope you?" *Help* comes from the Old English *helpen*—to aid—and the past tense is *hopa,* whose derivation may be the Indo-European word *hop*—to leap up in expectation. Who wouldn't help when they can hop, when they can jump for joy?

Sometimes helping is easy. My granddaughter stands at the head of the staircase and calls, "Mah!" That means, "Come quick and hold my left hand medium-lightly while I walk down the stairs. And don't pick me up. I only need a little help." I hope she can do it; in fact, I know she can. And, of course, I help.

Sometimes our hope is tested. My father fell and was in the intensive care unit of a Knoxville hospital. We arrived from Atlanta on March 11, 1993, just as snow began to fall in earnest over the city. Unknown to us, it was the beginning of a snowstorm of the century. This storm would dump over sixty inches on nearby Mount LeConte and paralyze much of the eastern United States for days.

We found Dad with a breathing tube in his throat and a chest tube in his side. He squeezed our hands and lifted his eyebrows in recognition. His doctor, speaking to us privately, outlined the situation. "You've got a ninety-year-old man with a punctured lung and moderate to severe lung disease. But he has a strong will to live. I am going to be aggressive unless you tell me otherwise."

Dad had always been in good health. The day before his fall, he drove to work just as he had done for seventy years. The fall broke three ribs, and air from a punctured lung inflated his body. But as they carried him to the ambulance, Dad asked for his hat, coat, and car keys. So I told the doctor, "Although he has had a full life, if he is still trying to breathe, help him to breathe."

My father's fight for life gave the doctor hope and encouraged him to help. We cheered Dad on, playing some of his favorite show tunes, like "You'll Never Walk Alone" from *Carousel*. "Walk on, walk on with hope in your heart, and you will never walk alone." We cheered the nurses, who were cut off from home and reinforcements by the snowstorm. They worked as long as they could, slept in an empty hospital room for a few hours, and then went on duty again. Hope and help went hand in hand.

Then more complications developed. Pneumonia in both lungs. Increased difficulty breathing. "Papa, you can do it," a granddaughter said. "But if you want to go home, that's all right." Dad fought on.

I spent the last night of winter with him, helping the respiratory therapists with the breathing treatments. Parts of it were not pretty. "What a wonderful profession," I told them. "Clearing the blockages so that people can breathe."

In the morning the doctor reported he was stable, and I rested while Alexandra took the afternoon shift. Then I heard her call, "You need to come. He doesn't look good to me." By the time I got to his room, nurses and doctors were running to help.

We were ushered into a critical care waiting room. We heard the sounds of urgent medical interventions, then quiet. We knew it was over. Lung punctured again. Respiratory failure. No hope. No help.

Through my father's death and the months that followed, I needed someone to *hope* me. And hope did come. The prayers and encouragement of many. A deepening awareness of the presence of God. A new way of being with my dad and a promise—"He will give you another Helper, a Comforter."[17]

My father died on the first day of spring, with the hope of resurrection and a new way to breathe in the air. My four-year-old grandniece drew a picture of flowers blooming, the sun shining. It was an Easter message: He is alive!

It's true. Sometimes the best help we can give is hope.

17 John 15:14.

Empty

One last trip with the pickup truck.
I left a few things
that no one
not even the junk man
wanted.

Footfalls on a bare floor
echo from the walls.
Our photographs once hung
from these empty nails.

A ceiling fan cools the room
but the child is long gone.
I am gone.
No one is here.

My father falls,
in a paralyzing snow.
The hospital crew,
a skeleton staff,
works overtime.

And then, just like that,
he is gone.

I take the long slow walk to the sterile room,
my footsteps echoing in the hall.
They have laid him here

To give us time to say good-bye.
It is his body, but the warmth is leaving.
He is not here,
only an empty shell.

The women walk early to the tomb
to pour fragrance on his tortured body.
The stone door is rolled to one side,
their footfalls echo on the dark rock walls.
There is flame and fire,
and blazing angels.
Why do you seek the living among the dead?

It is a question that comes
down through the years.
When we find the answer,
the death room becomes a birthplace,
and an empty space is filled.

Coats

First, my mother dies, and then, at the end of a long winter, my father. When we sell their prized homeplace, I end up with their winter coats. I make a plan to take them to downtown Atlanta, because I know it will be easy to find homeless people who need them. But I can't bring myself to give them away. The winter is cold and lonely. I need the warmth and security, the protection that my parents' coats represent. Yes, I have too many coats, but I am still not warm.

It is icy in our cabin in the North Georgia mountains. My mother's gray woolen coat hangs on a peg, and I wear it while I'm making the fire. It's a great fire-making coat, hip length, soft wool with reinforced buttons and three-quarter sleeves. I remember the fire my mother kept going in her bedroom when the nights were arctic-cold in Tennessee. Now her coat keeps out the mountain cold until the fire heats the stove. I feel warm and toasty.

That February I head to Washington, DC, for a National Prayer Breakfast event. I wear my father's U.S. Navy pea coat from World War II, a simple "working at sea" coat—tailored, dark, and proper—worn by naval officers on the ship's bridge. It's cold in the long, breezy halls of Congress, and there are many men wearing snappy double-breasted Navy coats with gold buttons and multistriped shoulder boards. I think to myself, *I bet none of them are wearing a coat that is from World War II, a coat that was worn by their dad.*

Alexandra and I visit the Holocaust Museum. The corridors are chilly, and I dread what I am about to see. I don't dare check my dad's coat. On the walls are massive murals with black-and-white photographs from concentration camps. It is winter, and you can feel the cold. The German guards wear long black coats; the Jewish prisoners are naked. Black coats and white skin. I want to give a naked man my coat.

In the year following my father's death, I start feeling better, warmer. I mourn less the loss of my father's "covering" and my mother's "caring." I'm able to share my warmth with others. I give my tan trench coat to Francis from Nairobi, who takes it to Brussels. I give my mother's fire-building coat to Meredith from the streets of Atlanta, and she looks great. Other friends come to visit from the Southern Hemisphere and need a warm coat for Atlanta's winter. Paulo from Rio wears my black coat to Washington, DC, and then back to Rio. Mardo from El Salvador gets my favorite Peruvian alpaca sweater.

Lester from Montego Bay, you will look good in my father's brown coat.

Marcos and Betty from Brasilia, come see us. You don't need to bring an overcoat.

There are plenty here to share.

There is life in a coat.
You can give it away or keep it.
Guard it or share it.
But keep one to build the home fires
and another with which to go to sea.

A question for all seasons: Is there anything that keeps you warm? And would sharing it make you warmer or colder?

Winter Solstice with Tornado

I am traveling in Brazil in the heat of summer. I have said good-bye to Brazilian friends who have shepherded me around the country and the vast interior state of Goias. Now I am traveling alone to the city of Sao Paulo, the largest city in Brazil and in the whole Southern Hemisphere.

I walk up the warm tarmac to the portable stairs of an aging jet. I try to fake it, as if I fly this route all the time, and ask the stewardess for a Brazilian paper. On the front is a photo of a dark twister in Crossville, Tennessee, a couple of hundred miles northwest of our family cabin. "That's too bad," I say to myself.

When I arrive home in Atlanta two mornings later, Alexandra says, "I think we should take a ride to our mountain cabin." A neighbor has called to say there has been a tornado, and a lot of trees have gone down. It feels like a call to come to the hospital. *Everyone is okay, but I think that you should come.*

We head up the mountain in silence, expecting I don't know what. Our Saab doesn't conquer the curves like you see in adver-tisements; instead, it hesitates before switching into a lower gear to take on the serpentine challenge. The first damage we see is a giant oak snapped off twenty feet from the ground. We round a bend, and there in the valley to our right lays a forest on its side, like an army of fallen soldiers too numerous to be buried. The silence is broken by the high-pitched roar of chain saws. What remains of the winter forest is brightened by the blue tarps that cover the roofs of our neighbors' homes. But the cabins seem strangely lonely without the protecting cover of their gray-bearded friends. The forest has fallen.

We make a right turn into what was a forested cul-de-sac.

Now it looks like a scene from World War I—the battle of the Argonne Forest. The trees are lying on their sides with their giant branches spreading everywhere. A tired, long-faced neighbor is dragging a branch away from his house.

"The work crews were two days cutting a path to your house," he explains. "Water was coming out the back. I hope there wasn't too much damage." Workers had turned the water off at the street but could not get down the driveway or into our house. Too many downed trees. "Let us know if we can help."

A crew of woodsmen helps us cut our way to the front door. There are shingles blown off, some broken windows and smashed gutters. The screens are riddled with holes created by acorns and even leaves that became flying missiles in the high wind. Otherwise, everything seems strangely intact. So I look at the good side. Five years of firewood. We weren't hit any harder. No one was killed.

But the days shorten and the darkness comes sooner. The volunteers have gone, and the fallen trees turn grayer and seem larger. The developer doesn't send help anymore, just directives that we are responsible to clean up our property. The work of cleanup becomes more solitary and heavy. The euphoria of being spared wears down and then off. I taste only a portion of what victims of disaster taste—deep-down fatigue, lack of resources, loneliness. Despair mixed with winter solstice.

But tomorrow the day will become longer and the darkness shorter. Each day will add sunlight. The appraiser will approve the repair to our roof and windows. A team of Latinos, who seem never to tire, will appear with chain saws. A man with a huge machine will lift fallen tree trunks like toothpicks. Spring will bring the first shoots of a new forest.

For now, I will sit on the porch, getting used to a new landscape. And I will think: What a view!

Setting Your Clock

It's switch time. We're changing from standard to daylight saving time—or is it the other way around?

I am never quite sure. On the Sunday morning after we make the change, I often don't know whether I'm an hour early or an hour late. Once my wife and I arrived at church just as they were singing the closing hymn. I kept my cool. "Just dropped by to see how you wrap things up," I told the preacher.

But I think I've got it now. Fall back in the fall. Spring forward in the spring. The next step is to learn how to use the funny little buttons on my watch so I can change the hour...

Scientists say that the body has a biological clock that can get out of sync when we set our internal clock to an external clock. Just off the interstate in downtown Atlanta, the 1996 Olympics countdown clock ticked for six years. Alexandra and I tried to ignore the clock as we drove by, but by the time it was under 365 days, we were on Olympic time.

Versions of a countdown clock are everywhere. Only 54 shopping days until Christmas! Start counting! Ten minutes to get to work! Out of my way! Drivers on the "late to work" clock close in on your bumper to get you on their schedules. (Don't let them tell you how to set your clock. Just get out of the way and let them go.)

When the kids were in school, it was the school year clock with its conflicting schedules that guided us. Vacations, marriages, parties, special events—they all had to be in sync with the children's calendar. Today, even as grandparents, we have to consult the school clock before we make plans.

How do I reset my internal clock so that it is not running according to someone else's schedule or sense of urgency? Part of the answer lies in recognizing the rhythm of the divine order of days and seasons.

> And God said, "Let there be lights in the expanse
> of the sky to separate the day from the night, and
> let them serve as signs to mark seasons and days
> and years."[17]

Whenever possible, let's reset our internal clock to the rhythm of the rising and setting sun and to the seasonal path of the earth as it orbits the sun.

This harmony came more naturally to the early Christian church. They tracked the liturgical year by the seasons, and the word *seasons* itself was derived from the Latin word *serere*—to sow. Easter was the time for the springing forth of dead seed; Pentecost for spring rains and rapid growth; fall for harvesting; Christmas was a season to be warm and protected.

If you don't like the way your clock is set, then reset it. Learn to listen to the earth's timepiece. Watch a tree's leaves change color. Throw acorns. Take a soaking bath or walk along the river. Lie on the grass and watch the clouds. Give the stars new names.

Drive by a cemetery and listen to your friends telling you to slow down.

---

17 Genesis 1:14.

Blockade Busters

"We need to go in and look around," my cardiologist, John Cantwell, says. On my previous visits, he has only listened, poked, prodded, and looked at the results of radioactive isotopes.

Go in? The two words a patient fears most. I try to suggest an alternative diagnosis. The discomfort around my chest? Probably gas. The cramping in my calf? A little more exercise, a little more stretching in the warm-up. Trust me, I want to say.

John looks at me skeptically. "Nevertheless, we need to take a look." He recommends a colleague skilled with a heart catheter.

Now I am rolling down the corridors of Piedmont Hospital in Atlanta. I try to make eye contact with well people who have come to see sick people. They look away but sneak a furtive glance at me as I roll by, like they are looking for signs of life. The gurney approaches a set of ominous double doors marked Cath Lab. "Tell him good-bye," the attendant says to my wife and daughters.

We roll through another set of double doors into a room that seems more like an operating theater than a laboratory. I am welcomed by three scrubbed and shiny girls in forest green robes. They look like they are still in college. *Maybe this is Rush Week.*

"Where does the head go?" I ask a technician. *No, silly, that's what you ask at the cemetery. Quick, change the subject.* I try to get on a first-name basis with the girls. *Should I ask their college and major, their hometown?* Before I can figure it out, the doctor arrives. His name is Charlie Brown III—really.

"We are going to have a look around. You can watch."

I'm given an injection, and I go to happy land, chatting and watching Dr. Brown spray some dye. Suddenly there are my insides for all to see. A block in the right coronary, left femoral, left thigh. "I know you came in for your legs, but they can wait," Dr. Brown says. "Let's start with the heart—tomorrow."

My first thought is denial. *This can't be me. I'm in good health. I take care of myself and exercise. Don't eat, drink, or smoke the bad stuff. Good genes.* But the proof is right there on the screen.

Before my angiogram, I stay busy, avoiding reflective thought and reading and writing little. *Better not to think about it.* Watch videos. My dreams are blank.

On the morning of my procedure, we roll into the same cath lab room. Different technicians—a little more serious. These are the blockade busters who will be going after the blockage in my right coronary artery. The doctor stands behind some kind of clear shield, manipulating the wire I see on the screen. I barely feel it going into my side.

"I am having a little trouble getting through," the doctor says. "This is more difficult than I expected."

His words wake me up! It is time to deal with God. *Don't send me upstairs to where they cut open your chest,* I pray. I think of the faith of some people whom Jesus touched. A leper—"If you want to, you can make me clean."[18] A father—"I believe, help my unbelief."[19] I remember the words of Jesus. "This is the work of God, to believe."[20] I visualize the wire breaking through, the blood flowing again.

"Are you okay?" a nurse asks.

18 Luke 5:12.
19 Mark 9:24.
20 John 6:29.

"Yes, I am believing for you. I am believing that you will break through!"

The doctor orders a different number of wire. I feel it slide into my side. He gives the artery a shake. I must have dozed. "We are through and inserting the stent now."

What a beautiful picture on the screen! A dark flow where previously there had only been a trickle. *Thank you, God.* Gratitude, relief, thankfulness—and a lesson about blocks and blockade busters. I was blocked and didn't know it. I needed someone to look, listen, and tell me there was a problem. Then I needed someone to help me get unblocked.

During my recovery, I ask God to show me the blocks in my life. I know I experience writer's block, but where else am I blocked? What impediments are in my life? How, concretely, am I kept from hearing God? I believe I will know as I take the time to listen.

This living metaphor keeps working in my mind. Where are the blocks in our city? Who is working on them? How do we get around them—or go through them?

And thank God for the blockade busters. Maybe you are one. Someone working quietly away at a blockage. Searching for a small hole or opening—without help, without much hope. A catheter is not a drill, just a wire that needs a foothold. Maybe your prayers, your quiet work, are making a small foothold, a little opening for someone else to make a breakthrough. Together we can quietly seek to work away at the blockages to the movement of the Spirit of God—in our own lives, in our neighborhood towns and cities, in our world.

Diminishment and Enhancement

I am a middle-aged man lying in a hospital bed, recovering from heart surgery and waiting for a few of my vitals to kick in. Three new directions impress themselves on my repaired heart, steps I would take if I were given more years to live.

First, I would spend more time with my wife and children and grandchildren. I would actively seek out their company, not just listen when they interrupt my important work.

Second, I would help find younger leadership for the non-profit organization I lead, the Atlanta Resource Foundation. Third, I would invest my time in passing on to the next generation what I learned about the grace of God.

Since making these resolutions, I have spent considerable time reflecting on the "diminishment and enhancement" that comes with growing older. This phrase comes from Dr. C. Gordon Cosby, the influential founding pastor of the Church of the Saviour in Washington, DC. He stopped his weekly preaching on the last Sunday of 2008, at the age of ninety-one.

After my surgery in 2004, Alexandra called him for some counseling. What could she do with a husband who was sometimes downhearted because he couldn't do all the busy things he used to do, because he had no identifiable project he was working on? Dr. Cosby told her that we were dealing with issues of diminishment and enhancement. "You have diminished strength and endurance, and you can't do all the things you used to think important."

"But there is also enhancement," he counseled. "You need to focus on that."

Enhancement! That was it. I started a list.

Pass the ball. What a thrill to pass the ball, to watch the receiver elude all defenders and take the ball in for a score. Perhaps the analogy of the handoff works even better. There is no greater joy than watching my successor at the Atlanta Resource Foundation take the ball and run like crazy with it. I have no regrets. Only support.

Cheer. Now is the time to cheer for others from the stands, from the bench. I don't have to be in on everything. It's time to bestow awards, not receive them.

Let *doing* come out of *being*. There is no amount of activity that can pump up a person who is not content with being. When all my doing is taken away, I am still a beloved, precious child of God. If I am centered in the Spirit within me, I can sit and watch a sunset. Though I am naturally gregarious, I can find fulfillment in quiet moments.

Give it away. Quite suddenly, I realized that I had accumulated too many possessions, and it became easier to give them away. Someone is going to carry all my stuff out of the house in a garbage bag. I'm going to give it away now to someone who can really use it.

When my grandmother was in her eighties she stopped shopping for Christmas and birthdays. Instead, she would give me one of her cherished old books and tell me about the author in great detail. Her inscription below her name made the book seem like a first edition. She taught me that giving is more than just cleaning out the house.

Just say no. It gets easier to say no, because I have said yes to fewer priorities. Even with the energy of a teenager, I could not attend all the banquets and fund-raising dinners to which we are invited. Instead I stop by to greet and leave (politicians have mastered this) or send my regrets with a check for the meal and then some. I am never turned down!

I don't answer the phone while eating dinner, watching a movie, or having an important conversation with my wife. If it's important, they will leave a message. After the fourth call from a girl reading from the same lines, my wife demanded that she identify her organization. "We do give to you once or twice a year, but we won't continue if you call back during dinner. Put that in your computer!"

Adopt a simpler creed. Some people lose their faith as they face the hardships of illness and growing old. But less can be more in this stage of life. My creed gets shorter. I really believe only a few things, but I believe them more deeply. Like my life depended on it. And it does.

Pain

Pain puts us on our back,
makes us depend on others,
brings us to our knees,
shortens our prayers to a single word. *Help!*

Pain helps us to measure our steps, our strength, our days,
to face the end of life with its decisions,
to use few words,
to bless our children, commend them to God,
and let them go.

Pain helps us keep short accounts,
to wait.
It keeps us from going, corresponding, calling, emailing.
It frees us to send messages by prayer.

Pain connects us with the groaning of the Spirit of God.
It condenses time,
becomes the great leveler,
makes us brothers and sisters with all who suffer,
all who have suffered,
and those whose suffering is over.

Pain makes us companions of Jesus along the path to
the cross.
Pain takes us from the Garden of Gethsemane,
to the courtyard of the Roman Empire,

to the hill of crucifixion,
to the coldness of the tomb.

Pain takes us to Easter morning,
Resurrection.

Pain ends.
Wake up one morning, and it's gone,
or find yourself in the new Narnia
or the new heaven,
and you can't feel your pain anymore.

Pain ends.
No kidding.

He Came to Me in a Dream

Vernon S. Broyles Jr. was the pastor of North Avenue Presbyterian Church in downtown Atlanta for many years. He was the mentor and father figure who kept me and many others going. I worked as a pastor under his direction. Even after he left for a mountain chapel, I called him up when I was in trouble or getting close to it. After his death, I had a conversation with him in a dream. I was pleased that he still referred to me as "young man."

Young man, you are not me and don't try to be.

Be yourself. You are not aware of how gifted you are and what a heritage you have.

You are not to be afraid of these people. They are bluffing you. You are much stronger than they. Outside, they look so powerful and proper, but inside, they are scared to death and looking over their shoulders to see who is gaining on them.

They will run you down if you act afraid of them, not because they are mean, but because they are afraid to see any sign of weakness in a leader. They fear this because they are so afraid of their own weaknesses tapping them on the shoulder.

What I am saying, young man, is that they are running scared, much more scared than you. You have as many gifts as they, but you are letting them push you around. I'm not talking about the outward accoutrements of power. I am talking about the inner qualities of real power, power that comes from God. And, young man, you have that. Never despise the gift of God that has been given you.

I'm not saying that you should go around being a little dem-agogue. No, be humble. Visit and care for the widow, the poor, the orphaned. Don't patronize them and don't expect them to do nothing. Call them to their best. Don't keep them dependent, doing your little religious stuff on them.

Now look at what you are doing in Jamaica and Brazil and the United Kingdom. Why, it is phenomenal! Don't walk around with your hands in your pockets, bemoaning that you have no one to help you. Call people together. Tell them what God is doing. Don't be afraid of religious bureaucrats, but get some ordinary people of faith together. Tell them what's going on and ask them to help.

God has put his hand on you, but you are afraid to claim the Spirit's authority. You are the son of the King. I'm not talking about being arrogant; you have a long ways to go before you get there. But you are acting afraid of powerful people. I was never afraid of them. If I had been, they would have run me out of town. These people look at your eyes, and, like a dog, they smell you. In the first minute, they know if they want anything more to do with you—you have either passed muster or they get rid of you. These powerful men are not looking for little rich boys; they've already got plenty of money. They are looking for sinew of the soul.

Don't waste your time with the lieutenants around them. Occasionally you will find one with heart. Be kind, care for them, but don't take them into your confidence. They are just *around* power; you *have* power.

Don't kowtow to any group in power or the people who seek its favor. Your favor comes from God. And don't spend too much time with religious leaders. Oh, you will find one here and there who will be a true friend, but most of them don't know what we are talking about. They are doing a religious power climb, talking about creating change but largely only writing articles and passing ecclesiastical motions.

Young man, *don't take everyone into your confidence.* Be kind to everyone, but it is no service to you, to your family, or to the kingdom of God for everyone to know your dreams, thoughts, weaknesses. Only a few have the right or even the background to know your soul. And don't waste time going to conferences; you've already learned all that you can from them.

As for your children, bring them into the dream, not to carry it, but to be enriched by it. They may be farther down that road than you realize.

Finally, have fun and go for it. Don't worry. If you need straightening out along the way, I'll be back.

The Gifts of the Gifted Child

When one of our daughters entered junior high, we were surprised and pleased to see how high she tested in verbal skills. She zipped through Latin, winning the top prize almost every year. In math, she was just okay, and in socialization skills, she tested on the lower end of the curve.

Although the school specialized in high-end students, this only meant that their lockstep curriculum was on a more accelerated level. Instead of trying to further develop our daughter's linguistic gifts, the school focused on improving her weaknesses. These weaknesses also became our central concern as parents.

While we all focused on her failures, our daughter stopped using big words in her vocabulary because other kids made fun of her. She quit raising her hand in English after the teacher said one too many times, "Does anyone else know the answer?" She soured on French when she and a friend had a difficult time in France. We wrung our hands.

If we could do it all over again, we would have majored on our daughter's gifts and not on her deficiencies.

As parents, almost all of us allocate valuable resources to encourage our children to work on their deficiencies so they can survive in this rough-and-tumble world. But we are learning from new research in child development that we need to concentrate our efforts where our children are strong, instead of spending all our money trying to improve their weaknesses. Eventually, our children may be able to develop enough of their less-gifted side to at least get by in this world.

My brother was raised in football Big Orange Country. In the eighth grade he went to a boarding school crazy over sports. Unfortunately, he could not throw a football or catch one. Fortunately, he had an art teacher who, while he couldn't tell the difference between a football and a baseball, knew artistic talent when he saw it.

Knowing my older brother, I was totally surprised when I saw him as a college student diving well in a crowd of athletic boys. He was not the most acrobatic, but he was the most artistic. In pool tag, he dove under the opposition like a speeding torpedo, and he was almost always the last man out. I was even more surprised to see how well he learned to play tennis as an adult.

The needs of a growing family compelled my brother to spend most of his adult life as a business executive. And while business was never his first love, he was successful because he knew how to gather a team of people around him—even and especially his wife—who were extremely skilled in their fields. He had learned not only how to compensate for his weaknesses but to develop new strengths.

I am sure that my parents had wrestled with two obvious issues: How can an artist survive? Who will run the family business? Those were not easy questions to answer back then, and parents still struggle over them today. But when we finally sold the family company in his middle age, my brother devoted more time to painting, his first love. He was able to go back to school and develop the gifts he was not allowed to pursue as a young person.

Most gifted people often have glaring and even fatal flaws. "Not every golfer has every club in the bag," said pro golfer Lee Trevino. I have known people who are extremely gifted speaking to large groups and totally flat in ordinary conversation. "He's a brilliant communicator but really disappointing one on one," said a crestfallen man about a mutual friend. I told him the Lee Trevino story.

Golf, like school, rewards the well-rounded game, but some of us have to try to hit the long shot with the wrong club. Maybe if we only have a 5-iron, we will have to drive with it, pitch with it, and putt with it until we believed we are the best 5-iron person in the country club, and maybe the city, and who knows, maybe the state. Then gradually, perhaps we will become open to adding a 6-iron and a 4-iron, and a 7 and so on.

The brilliant Albert Einstein was portrayed as the quintessential absent-minded professor. But when he was teaching at Princeton, the university hired a team of people to remove and replace the chalkboard when he had finished covering it with his writing and equations. The university did not want him erasing anything. Instead, they sprayed the board with shellac and kept it for further study.

I have had professors who were not able to get to and from class without a spouse to drive and guide them. While we admire the brilliance of these impractical teachers, we also make fun of them and speak about them in condescending ways. Many schools are guilty of giving awards and tenure to their most congenial teachers while overlooking the eccentric but brilliant people in their midst.

A generation after my daughter went through junior high, we have a grandson entering the seventh grade. He is gifted in math and science but weaker in socialization skills. We try to find a school or a path where he can survive long enough to value his unique giftedness. Is there an academic community where he can learn to get by in the areas where he is so obviously deficient? Perhaps one day he will even excel in social skills.

These gifted people, like my daughter and grandson and brother, are our family and national treasures. It behooves all of us to recognize, believe in, encourage, and preserve the gifts of the gifted. Leave the lockstep tests and programs to the average. Let's live with a little eccentricity. These people can get their ball to the green and into the cup with whatever club they choose—just in a little different way.

When they putt out, I'll send up a much-needed cheer. Great 5-iron!

Bad Tired

My granddaughter is so tired she got bad.
Surely you've known a child who was so tired she was bad.
I thought it just happened to children,
but tonight my wife said,
"I'm so tired. Tell me that I am not bad."
That seemed strange.
"No, you are not bad. You are just tired."

Then it was my turn.
I cleaned the kitchen.
I paid the bills.
But I did not write my thank-you letter
or finish doing my taxes.
There must be something wrong with me, I thought.

How silly to link tiredness and badness.
When did we begin to think the call of sleep bad?
Did we lose omni-awakeness when we lost Paradise?
I don't know.
But I am going to sleep in the arms of Jesus,
Abba Father.

Good tired. Good night.

Shout: Birrrth!

"My wife have baby. No speak Inglis. Please come hospital. Quick."

Alexandra and I rush to the hospital to help a young Brazilian couple. We met them at a local church, and since they were alone in a large city, we told them to let us know if we could help. We remember what it is like to be in a country without family and without command of the language.

Now in response to their appeal, we are racing together down the hall of a hospital to the maternity ward. Alexandra is ushered into a small birthing room. I'm told to wait outside in the hall. I eavesdrop.

"Tell her that she needs to sign these papers," the birthing nurse commands Alexandra. One paper gives the medical staff permission to draw blood from the infant, another absolves the hospital of all responsibility in case something goes wrong. Yet another is for circumcision if the baby is a boy.

Alexandra translates and then joins me at the door.

"Is that it?" I ask hopefully.

"No. We wait till birth."

We chat and wait. Pray and wait. Hours go by. There is no switch to dim the fluorescent lights in the waiting room. It is impossible to get comfortable. The steel armrests of the blue plastic chairs are welded together—maybe they think someone wants to steal them. I try rolling up in fetal position, but the armrest whacks my head. I twist and slide my arms and legs until I am lying under the armrests of three chairs. My nose whacks the underside of the metal bar. I could use a pillow but—help! How do I get out? Eventually I extricate my tangled limbs and steal enough pillows from a nearby room to build a suspension bridge between the armrests. I look like the man in the moon in a waxing crescent.

I doze off and find myself in the land of memories. May 1968. I am in a maternity waiting room in Brazil. It is hot. Alexandra is in delivery. The doctor walks into the waiting room and says in broken English, "Maybe we take baby if things no speed up. Maybe we change the baby's blood. But no problem."

Then it is a year earlier. I am sitting close to the floor on a broken-down couch in the two-room shack of a very poor Brazilian family. I have brought a midwife to help a young mother give birth. On the other side of the curtain, the midwife is delivering the baby, with no anesthesia for the mother. I feel useless—except I did deliver the midwife. There are screams, followed by the cries of a baby. Birrrth!

Just before 5:00 a.m. someone jostles me awake. "Your wife wants you to come. It is time."

The team is assembled in the birthing room. The husband is on one side; his wife's friend on the other. The birthing nurse is in the middle. My wife is holding the expectant mother's hand. I am posted outside the door—for what I do not know.

"Push," the nurse encourages.

"Impurre!" my wife echoes in Portuguese.

A slow eternity of time passes. A cry. Several cries. The nurse pops out of the room and yells down the hall. "Birrrth!" She reminds me of a soccer coach yelling "Gooooal!"

I am not going to cry. No, I am not. This is an everyday occurrence. I go in the room, and the father is grinning from ear to ear. "It's a boy, and his name is Kevin," he announces. Tears fall down my cheeks.

A few weeks later, Alexandra and I are sitting around the house, waiting for a call from our son-in-law. He is going to tell us when to come to the hospital for the birth of our third grandchild. Nothing is happening, we have been told. It will be midafternoon.

At 1:30, our son-in-law Keith calls. "1:29," he says.

"Birrrth!" I cry. It is a boy, and his name is John Thomas.

Kevin and John Thomas, a first- and a fifth-generation American born just weeks apart. They arrive just in time for a new century, surrounded by a team of people all working together to give them birth. Together, they are a new generation of hope and leadership potential coming into the world. They point to the power of a birthing team to bring fresh vitality into the world—a human life, an idea, a vision, a mission.

Another Kind of Birth, Sorely Needed

Our cities, countries, and world are badly in need of new leadership, new ideas, new birth. For these world-changing ideas and leaders to come into their own, they need some of the same supportive roles and functions that physical birth requires.

Some of us are **mothers** able to go through the process of conception, gestation, waiting, heaviness, pain—until the seed takes life, then joy!

Some are **fathers** able to provide love, security, place, seed, encouragement, nurture.

Some are **midwives** able to help others bring forth new life that they could not give birth to alone.

Some are **translators** able to tell others what is going on.

Some are **announcers** who recognize new life when they see it and proclaim to the world: "Birrrth!"

Together, we are the birthing team—the critical mass getting behind the risk-taking visionaries. We understand our role and value the roles of others—even if they are just standing in the hall. Not all of us can be mothers or fathers. Not every creative idea that arises in our community has to come from us. Some of us just need to stand and cheer!

Find your role and cherish it.

Blossom and Blessed

No visit to Kingston, Jamaica, is complete without visiting Father Richard Ho Lung and the Missionaries of the Poor who live and work near the docks of the old part of the city. Father Ho Lung is famous and courageous, and his community cares for the sick, the dying, and the discarded.

Father Ho Lung is also a musician, composer, and prophet. When no one else speaks out, he calls the nation to account for its sins. He once confronted the owner of a hedonism club that was promoting mass nude weddings as a way to attract tourists from affluent countries. We pray for him.

"Would you like to see some of our family?" he asks. A brother from the community, a priest in training from the Philippines, Father Henry Lozano, rides with us through streets that look like alleys. We pass a truck stripped of everything but its frame, and then we come to a compound protected by a Rust-Oleum–colored metal gate. An eye peers through a peephole, and the gate swings open. We are suddenly in another world, a Caribbean garden of exotic flowers and fruit-bearing trees.

But the real treasure is the people. A young girl comes to meet me and takes my hand. She leads me around to meet people. Her face looks like an underinflated soccer ball that has been kicked in, and her smile covers a mess of teeth going in all directions.

"Shirley is epileptic, and we have to watch her in case she falls," Henry explains. "Sometimes she falls to get attention."

"I am paying lots of attention," I tell Shirley. "So don't fall on me."

Henry takes a cuddly baby girl in his arms. "This is Blessed," he says. "Her mother has AIDS, but Blessed has tested negative."

He takes me to a room for AIDS mothers lying on two long rows of cots. "We have lost two hundred mothers to AIDS in the last two years."

A priest is reading from *Our Daily Bread* to a tiny indentation under a blanket. "This is Blossom, the mother of Blessed," Father Henry whispers. "She is in her last days. A family from Atlanta is going to adopt Blessed."

We walk over to the bed, and Father Henry introduces me to the bundle that is the mother of Blessed. The blanket moves. A head appears. Blossom slowly gets herself up on an elbow.

"Do you know the Mullins in Atlanta?" she asks. She is studying me with piercing eyes.

"No," I say. "But I will try to meet them."

I know that, realistically, this quick response may just be a nervous reaction. Maybe I will meet the new parents of her children and maybe I won't. We pray together, and Blossom holds on to me as if her life depended on it.

As we drive back through the broken-down community to catch my plane, I ask Henry where the patients of the Missionaries of the Poor get their drugs.

"People like you bring Advil and Tylenol from the United States."

"No, I mean AIDS medicine."

"We don't have any medicine to treat AIDS," he says. "We can only treat the accompanying diseases."

I am on the plane awaiting takeoff, but my mind and heart are back with Blossom and Blessed. The Missionaries of the Poor may not be able to treat AIDS, but they know how to treat the underlying condition—the need for living and dying human beings to be treated with love and dignity.

I fly away to Atlanta. Blessed will soon follow me, and her mother, Blossom, will fly away to glory.

Lightning Strike

The sky is clear. It is May 6, 1991, and my daughter Julie and I are almost back to the house from a walk around the neighborhood. Suddenly my wife, Alexandra, yells from the house, "Something terrible has happened to Emmit Young! He was killed in an automobile accident in Brazil."

I run to the house, too stunned to take in the news. Alexandra tells me that there has been a brief wire service report about a missionary from Atlanta killed in Brazil. A fellow missionary has called to confirm that it is Emmit, a great personal friend and my colleague in ministry. He is a cofounder and secretary of the Atlanta Resource Foundation. He and his wife, Sandy, are among our dearest friends.

Emmit had already survived one head-on collision with a drunk driver going the wrong way on a freeway in Brazil. He was not expected to survive, but he did. At the invitation of Wayne Smith, the founder of Atlanta's Friendship Force, Emmit went on to work with government leaders in Brazil. We had teamed up when he was home on furlough and had worked together for years.

"Sandy is home alone," Alexandra said. "We need to go there right now, before she hears the news all by herself."

As we drive the twenty miles between our homes, I rehearse what I am going to say. How will I break the news that I am still unable to believe? Is this how military chaplains feel, driving to the home of a new widow?

Sandy is waiting for us at the carport door. She already

knows; her pastor has told her. In one blinding head-on strike, her husband and our friend is gone. He was thrown out the back of a car, never to regain consciousness in this world again.

✦ ☿ ✦

Family and friends of all sizes gather at the Youngs' home. We run out of things to say. Emmit's granddaughter and I take a break to explore her grandfather's vegetable garden in the backyard. We pick one strawberry after another, tasting them carefully, looking for the sweetest one. The gardener is gone, but the fruit remains.

Emmit's body arrives from Brazil to a mortuary on Spring Street in downtown Atlanta. Brazil has a twenty-four-hour interment law, and his friends and coworkers have worked tirelessly to get through mountains of red tape to prevent his immediate burial in Brazil. Then, at great personal cost to themselves, they have flown his body to Atlanta.

I look down at my friend. The only mark is a raised bump on his temple. I tell him good-bye.

✦ ☿ ✦

It is evening, and the smell of storm is in the air. A month after Emmit's death, we are in a condo perched on a ridge above the Great Smoky Mountains National Park. Through the large plate-glass windows we watch a parade of massive thunderheads. There is lightning dancing back and forth between them, and each cloud appears darker and more furious than the one before.

Our daughter Julie calls from Atlanta. "Mom, Dad, the house has been hit by lightning. It blew up the television and knocked the electrical plates off the walls. Yes, Bootsie and I are okay. The fire department is on the way." Bootsie was our courageous Lhasa who once chased an entire herd of deer in the North Georgia mountains.

In one blinding strike, perhaps two, lightning had traveled through the top of our most prized tree, a 150-year-old tulip poplar, and hit two large oak trees. Then it had raced through the tool shed and the lawn mower, followed a wire into the house, ran through the television, phones, refrigerator, and circuit breakers, and finally exited to the ground. All in a matter of seconds, and all around, under, and over Julie and Bootsie.

I hug a gigantic tulip poplar in the Smoky Mountain park to measure its girth. It has a terrible gash from a lightning strike, but over the years, it has healed itself. There is hope. "Perhaps we can save our tree," I say to Alexandra.

"You don't understand," the tree surgeon says. "Your tulip poplar is split three times from top to bottom. The question is, can we save your house?"

The trees were felled.

The refrigerator and TV were replaced.

But there's a big hole in the woods.

We are thinking about planting a garden. Does anyone know which plants grow in the shade?

I Mourn Your Fall

Emmit Young (1940–1991)

I mourn your fall.
You who came to life in Pennsylvania soil,
who grew strong and tall in Brazilian rain,
reached wider and grew deeper
in Georgia clay.

Gone is the friend
who shared my past present future.
We grew together.
I stand exposed,
alone.

Acorns fall on the woodland floor,
some will die and some will grow.
Trees already here will mature in your light.
In time, they will cover the hole where once you were.

You have fallen, my friend,
but you left behind a forest.

Emmit Young was a friend, co-laborer, and counselor. He was
Latin to the core. He taught us that when all is hopeless, God is
present even in that hopelessness—and doing something new.

Those That Guard Treasures
Turn into Dragons

I am lying on the massage table, feeling the tightness as usual in my neck and left shoulder. The masseuse tells me that the tightness is cumulative, brought about by years of injuries, tension, and working muscles incorrectly.

In a state of semi-consciousness, I think back to extremely difficult wrestling matches in high school and on the YMCA team. I recall a track injury to my Achilles tendon, football injuries to my knee and hamstring.

As the masseuse continues to work up and down my body, I remember illnesses, old wounds, past hurts. I remember how my mother and father cared for me, and I quietly sob. It is as if the Spirit is working out old memories, relaxing their kinks and enabling me to let them go.

I thank the masseuse for taking me through my life and helping me get rid of some old and painful memories that my body was holding in. She is totally surprised by my response, and I never have the same experience again.

It starts me wondering. If and when we finally go to be with God, are all the accumulated pains and hang-ups and sins worked out of us over time? Or is the change instantaneous? Some sacred texts point one way; some another. Some suggest remembrance for deeds done in the body; others a brand-new life completely disconnected from the old.

In *The Voyage of the Dawn Treader* by C. S. Lewis, Eustace, the spoiled brat, runs off in Narnia, leaving behind his siblings and friends so he can claim a horde of gold and jewels all for himself. Since he has not read any fairy tales, he does not know that those who guard treasures turn into dragons. He is surprised, then alarmed, when he touches his skin and realizes that it is scaly. His worst fear is realized. He has turned into a dragon.

As the story unfolds, he repents and promises not to be a selfish dragon any longer. He will reform. He begins to pull the scales from his skin. It hurts so he pulls slowly, like taking off a Band-Aid. Aslan, the great lion from beyond the sea, appears and asks if he would like help. "You have not gone deep enough," he explains. Aslan begins the work of freeing Eustace from the dragon scales, and he digs his claws much deeper than the boy expects. The pain is overwhelming, but in the end Eustace is in his own skin again.

I am afraid that God's surgery to give me a new heart and new body is much deeper work than I thought.

Jars of Clay

I step gingerly through a broken window into the dusty and dangerous darkness of an abandoned and broken-down church. The congregation had moved to a safer neighborhood, and the building has become a crash pad for junkies.

"Hello!" Anita Favors yells. "Coming through!" Anita is the copastor of a new ministry for the homeless, Jars of Clay, and she is giving fair warning to anyone who might be lurking in the building.

"Watch your step," she shouts back to me.

I walk forward in the darkness, lifting my feet high with each step as if I'm walking through a cow pasture. I don't want to step on a mattress or dirty clothes or an empty syringe.

"Look at the burn marks on the pews," Anita points out. "That's where the addicts heated their crack cocaine. But look at the large wooden cross on the wall. They didn't touch it!

"Can you imagine what this place will look like when we clean it up and have homeless families in here?"

I can imagine, but I cannot yet see what she sees. I salute her as a visionary who sees a garden in garbage.

I enjoy these personal visits to a ministry in its initial stages. Then we can return months later and see the after. Each month, we take a group of professionals, businesspeople, and ministry folks out of their comfort zones to experience something of what the Spirit of God is doing in an impoverished corner of Atlanta. The group is called City Lights, and we often visit old buildings in various stages of renovation. We listen to visionaries paint the picture, and then we come back again to see their steady progress toward the fulfillment of their dreams.

I wrote a poem about my visit with Anita to this shell of a church, which in just a few months was to become a shelter, a place of refuge and healing for homeless women and their children. My poem is in honor of all the brave men and women everywhere who see in an old, empty, dilapidated building a vision of loveliness—a space where God's children can be reborn.

Full House

Desolate lonely cross
towering over filth and slime.
Where broken, angry addicts eliminated,
resolute feminine hands now gather the grime,
scour floors, pews, and walls
with their sweat and tears,
decontaminate.

They sand, paint, and pray
for strength, skill, and help.
First a trickle:
a plumber, an electrician, an architect.
A dollar here and a dollar there.
Then a flood,
five dollars, ten, fifteen, and twenty,
volunteers pour in by the score,
a contractor, a beautician, a counselor.

A roof is painted, then a fence.
On the ceiling over clean, well-made beds,
red, yellow, green zoo animals dance for joy.

Now they come into their Father's House
The old and the young,
men and women, mothers and fathers
with their children.
They come from other empty buildings
from under bridges
first-timers and lifers of the street
gather under a new roof.

The vision is fulfilled
My House is full
My joy complete.

When Anger Stalks

Atlanta 1999. It is a hot Thursday in July. The temperature reaches ninety-five degrees. At 2:50 p.m., Mark O. Barton starts to get even. He shoots and kills nine people across from my office building, injuring thirteen more. The victims have nowhere to go. They are face to face with an enraged man determined to kill every person he sees who seems to be happy and successful.

For those left behind to think about the implications of implacable anger, I offer these guidelines.

First, **make certain anger is not stalking within.** Anger has a way of finding anger. It goes after it like a heat-seeking missile, finds itself, and wants to destroy itself. When workers in the US civil rights movement went out to face an angry crowd, they were counseled to get rid of any hatred they were feeling. "Pray for those who despitefully use you."[21] It was practical advice, a way of trying to be safer in the face of extreme anger.

Conversely, I have found myself most at risk when I have insisted on acting as a policeman, attempting to enforce my set of rules and regulations on others. Anger, even veiled anger, begets anger.

Second, **get out of anger's way.** Don't try to be a hero. Mark Barton started shooting, and a security consultant said, "Run! If you can't run, hide." I've read that martial arts instructors teach their students to run first and fight only as a last resort, when faced with corporal danger.

Likewise, when I am being tailgated, my wife counsels me

21 Luke 6:28.

not to hit the brake but to exit the scene, even if I have to pull the car off the road. "But I am in front, going five to ten miles faster than the speed limit. I will not be forced to go faster." My rights are not the issue. Getting out of the way of implacable anger is.

Third, when anger is in your face, **consider feigning disinterest.** A friend who is a psychiatrist asked a group of professional thieves serving time how they picked their victims. "Easy," they said. "The one who is afraid." Who do they avoid? "The one who is disinterested. You can never tell how they will react."

In the movie *Saving Private Ryan,* a group of soldiers argue about whether their captain, played by Tom Hanks, should have ordered an attack on a German machine-gun position when it wasn't part of the mission to save Ryan. Men were lost in the successful effort. While the men argue, Hanks appears disinterested. When urged to do something by one of his men, he responds, "I wonder how the Dodgers are doing? Last I heard…" Not interested.

In 1994 I was walking with my wife and a colleague on the Copacabana Beach in Brazil. I noticed the Southern Cross in the darkening sky and looked up to admire it. At that moment, I was knocked to the sand. A man stood over me with a hunting knife and said, in good English, "Money or I kill you." He had several friends with him.

I started fighting him with my feet and was only saved from being stabbed by my wife, who shouted in Portuguese, "The blood of Jesus is powerful. Leave in the name of Jesus!" She turned to me, still lying on the sand and commanded, "Stand up and claim the name of Jesus." I did. She took the taxi money out of her socks and threw it at the thieves. The wind picked up the bills and blew them away. The would-be robbers ran after the money and kept running. Alexandra was not afraid. She acted unpredictably.

While living in Brazil, I noticed a police officer at a busy intersection writing down the license numbers of cars that ran the stoplight. He had a motor scooter, and I asked him why he didn't give chase.

"First," he said, "I will have trouble catching them with that scooter. Second, if I do catch them, they will be mad, and I will be mad. There will be words. They may kill me. I may kill them. It's easier to write down their tag number. When they go to pick up their tag next spring, they will have a ticket and a fine."

As a volunteer at the Atlanta federal penitentiary, I once asked the chaplain which prisoners were the easiest to reform. "Murderers who committed crimes of passion," he said. The psychotic killers who could murder without hatred were not likely to change. People who committed a crime of passion could more easily let their feelings go and learn to live in a different way. "Then you have a reformed murderer," the chaplain explained.

When anger stalks, we need to do an internal check on our own anger. We need to become aware of our own aggression. Then if we can, we need to move out of the way. Get off the road. Throw money into the wind. Do not be afraid, for God is our protector and judge.

Small Help

I'm not going to help him or give money to her project, because the needs are too great. My little will do no good.

How many times have we said that? The trend in philanthropy is focused on large gifts rather than many scattered, smaller gifts. The goal is significance and effectiveness. It is the task of the fund-raiser to convince donors of their importance. What a difference your gift makes! Your help is bigger, better, more effective!

I want to say a word for the small and insignificant, the "ineffective" gift.

Certainly it is naive to believe that one organization or cause will solve all ills. It's just not true. But fund-raisers know how busy, goal-oriented people think, and organizations often pitch their presentations to a simplistic way of looking at the world and its challenges. Alas, life is just not that simple, and the problems are much more entrenched.

A Kenyan couple who attended our church lost their daughter. The funeral was in Kenya, and they needed to send a family member home to represent them and to pay the medical bills and burial expense. I mentally estimated their expenses. They would never be able to cover them. What good would my gift do? Then I was invited to a *harambee* at the couple's apartment. *Harambee* means "all pull together" in Swahili. Everybody helps out a little. Guess what? The group not only sent a family member to Kenya but covered all the medical and funeral expenses.

"Sometimes people in the United States are reluctant to get

involved with someone in need because they are overwhelmed by the need," a Kenyan pastor studying in Atlanta told me. "In Kenya we *know* that we can't do it all, so we do what we can. Others do what they can. When the people in need see how many people are pulling together to help them, *harambee,* they are so encouraged, they get back on their feet."

Most of us don't have the resources to give big gifts, so let's think small. Let's give a word of encouragement or a compliment. We'll let another car in line when we ourselves are in a hurry. We can write a short note or a quick email. We can send in our small donation.

My church has a worship service for the homeless. I always cry when the offering is passed. I watch destitute men and woman put their quarters and dollar bills in the offering plate. Sometimes one of them even gives a ten- or twenty-dollar bill. Just as when Jesus took five loaves of bread in his hands and multiplied them,[22] a funny kind of mathematics happens. There is "good measure, pressed down, running over."[23] The blessings keep coming, and small gifts gradually become bigger small gifts.

Let's jump up and down for the small donor. Think small. Give small and often.

22 Matthew 14:13–21; Mark 6:30–44; Luke 9:10-17; John 6:5–15.
23 Luke 6:38.

Alphaville

Alphaville. Would you like to live there?

I can still see this gated, secure community in my mind. It has four locked gates. The rest of the property is enclosed by a chain-link fence that is topped by razor wire. The security system is state of the art. With a mechanical voice, it demands that I identify myself. Fortunately, I have a security clearance.

The household help and construction workers have a lower level of clearance. They are searched by a security guard whenever they leave the property so the homeowner doesn't have the awkward task of frisking a maid or a plumber.

The kids have it made. They can ride their bikes to the ice cream parlor and leave them unchained. Alphaville is close to expensive private schools, so children can get to school safely and quickly. If parents are in a pinch to get to work on time—the center of the city is relatively close—they can rent a helicopter taxi at the helipad.

Alphaville sounds like science fiction, but it's a real community just seven and a half miles from Sao Paulo, Brazil. Sao Paulo is a city of eighteen million—with problems. Some of its criminals have grown tired of simple burglary and now specialize in kidnapping for ransom. They are not interested in killing the victim, just collecting the money. To underscore the reality of their threats, they may send the victim's family a finger or an ear. The rich pay.

"I don't want to live in a place like this, but I have to think first of my children's security," a parent told a *Washington Post* reporter.[24]

Places like Alphaville are not new. We've had our castles, towers, and forts, and, naively, we thought society had out-grown them.

I was jolted back to reality when a Sao Paulo family called me to ask if Atlanta was safe for their high-school-age son. He was driving around the United States. Could he get a motel where he would not be robbed in the night? Could he drive down the streets without being held up at a stoplight and losing his car? I had forgotten that people in much of the world, including in neighborhoods in the United States, must think about the safety of themselves and their children every hour of every day.

Sometimes I introduce myself as a person working to mix people up, someone "stirring the pot." The Atlanta Resource Foundation is designed to help people engage with ministries and nonprofits outside of their zip code and comfort zone. We care about jobs, transportation systems, affordable housing, and access to medical care. We want livable neighborhoods and excellent public education, honest police officers, and a capable criminal justice system. And don't forget open spaces, lakes and streams and rivers, and public services for immigrants.

Those of us who live in some version of Alphaville must learn to want for all what we want for ourselves. More than ever it is essential that we know about each other and care for one another across our fortress walls. Our very survival depends on it.

---

24 Anthony Faiola, "Brazil's Elites Fly Above Their Fears: Rich Try to Wall Off Urban Violence," *Washington Post,* June 1, 2002.

Fate of Fences

The United States is investing a lot of our limited financial resources into building a fence to keep out unwanted immigrants. How, I wonder, have fences fared throughout human history?

The Great Wall of China was built in just two thousand years. The Mongols came over it and around it. Today it's a good tourist attraction.

The walls of Troy lasted until the Trojans were overcome with curiosity and took in the wooden horse.

The walls of Jericho came atumblin' down.

The walls around Jerusalem were breached.

The wall around Masada was pretty good until the Romans built a ramp.

The walls of Rome could not keep out the barbarian hordes.

The Dutch built a wall but could not keep the English out of the territory that today we call Manhattan. The remains of the wall were paved over by Wall Street.

Then there was the wall at the Alamo. Remember the Alamo?

The Maginot Line, a massive line of fortifications on the border between Germany and France, did not keep the Germans out of France in World War II.

The Atlantic Wall that Erwin Rommel built on behalf of Adolf Hitler could not keep the Allies out of Fortress Europe.

The Berlin Wall lasted twenty-eight years. A famous American president said, "Mr. Gorbachev, tear down this wall!" Now you can buy pieces of it for souvenirs.

"Something there is that doesn't love a wall."

—Robert Frost

Water Wars and the Well of Life

It is 6:30 Sunday morning. I am outside, watering our wilting landscape before the ban against daytime watering kicks in. We have just rescued our fertile soil from billowing waves of English ivy, and in its place, we've planted ferns, azaleas, and rhododendron. I can only water on even-numbered days. It is 2001, and our imagined fears of catastrophic social disruption at the end of the millennium have been replaced by real drought. Maybe on odd days I will use the water we stored for Y2K to try and save some plants.

For now, I am dipping into my community's receding water supply. While I water our garden, the state's largest lakes are dwindling to mud flats. The US Army Corps of Engineers has made a mistake in reading water levels, and they have released a record amount of water from the state's largest reservoir, Lake Lanier. The water is traveling down to Alabama and Florida. With the lake at its lowest level since it was first filled—at the end of World War II—the war between the states for water is heating up.

In previous decades, water has been so plentiful in Atlanta that we cannot imagine the city without its manicured green lawns, borders of lush azaleas and dogwoods, and wooded lots of towering pine and hardwood trees. Now, Georgia farmers are losing their crops. Should I really be concerned about a few ornamentals? As I walk through the yard with my hose, drooping leaves and bent stalks thank me like thirsty refugee children whose cups are being filled by relief workers.

I think back on a flight I made to Lima, Peru. I was looking down at the lush Andean jungle and snow-capped mountains when suddenly all I could see were mountains that had turned to gray dust.

"What happened?" I asked my travel companion in disbelief.

"We are on the western slope where it does not rain."

Over dinner in Lima, our hostess told me about her project called Trees Lima. The next day I looked for her trees on the boulevard. I found them, newly planted and supported by wires in the gray median. A man bearing a five-liter tin can on his back gave them a drink. I learned that the Shining Path guerrilla movement had deepened the water crisis by blowing up water mains and downing electric power lines. Anything green had been watered by men with tin buckets on their shoulders. Will this be our future in Atlanta?

I remember my trip two weeks earlier to the Brazilian city of Manaus where the Amazon River is formed by the confluence of the Solimoes and Negro Rivers. Here the mighty Amazon was so wide that I couldn't see across it. In some other places, it was fifty kilometers from one bank to the other. The river had not yet crested, and the mud and water stains on the trees showed that it had another two meters to climb. With 230,000 cubic meters of water sweeping by each second, the trees and their islands would disappear for weeks at a time.

I think of all the ancient cities that were built around water sources—a well, a river, a lake. I think of Lima, where squatter villages often developed around a well or cistern with a single spigot of water that might or might not be clean. Then I think of Jesus at that ancient well in Samaria dug by the servants of

Jacob.[25] It is high noon. He is thirsty, the well is deep, and he has no bucket and no rope. A woman is drawing water.

"Give me a drink," Jesus says. She is surprised that a member of the ruling class would ask a woman of a lower, mixed-race caste for a drink from her bucket.

For Jesus and the woman at the well, water becomes a metaphor for a source of inner strength. "The water that I will give will become in them a spring of water gushing up to eternal life."[26] Jesus spoke of this revitalization of the inner being as being born again, as the bread of life, as a new heart.

I finish watering the fragile plants in my care. In drought and in plenty, I realize, I must take time to sit down beside the well of life. I must keep it clean and drink slowly from its living waters. Then I must build my life around it.

What in your life serves as a well of living water? How can you keep it clean, and what would it mean to sit beside it, to build your life around it?

25 John 4:4–26.
26 John 4:14 (NRSV).

Fly, Thunderbird, Fly

It was a very special car, a road car. If any car deserved the title Thunderbird, it was this 1961 cream-colored, two-door automobile with a gleaming white hardtop. Vital statistics: a 390-cubic-inch V-8 engine, 300 horsepower, a four-barrel Holley carburetor with dual exhausts.

My father bought it for five thousand dollars in 1961 from the same Cincinnati specialty shop that customized the cars of President John F. Kennedy. It weighed in just forty-two pounds short of two tons, and with its low profile and sleek fantail body, the car seemed to be begging for a full-throttle road test on the Utah salt flats. When it built up a little speed, you could let up on the pedal, and the car's momentum would still carry it—blazing fast—down the highway.

My father needed an excuse to see what his brand-new Thunderbird could do, so he and my mother drove from Knoxville to Pensacola, Florida, where Alexandra and I were serving in our first pastorate. Years later I found their marked-up AAA map. They went down US 11 to Chattanooga, up Lookout Mountain toward Monteagle, down a newly constructed stretch of I-59 toward Alabama, around Montgomery on US 231, and on to Evergreen, where a new stretch of I-85 had just been completed.

My mother went to sleep somewhere south of Chattanooga and did not wake up until they pulled into our sandy driveway, just off the bay near the Pensacola Naval Air Station. "The Thunderbird felt like it coasted down from the Smoky

Mountains clear to the white sand beaches of the Gulf of Mexico," my father reported.

When Dad died in 1993, I got the car. It broke down twice just driving it from Knoxville to Atlanta. That should have been my signal. Like a retiring thoroughbred, the Thunderbird had grown accustomed to the care of a seasoned mechanic. I finally got it to Atlanta and had great hopes of tinkering with it and wheeling around the city on Saturday mornings. But the T-Bird was made for the open road and not the darting, pushing, grinding traffic of Atlanta. I took it to the office a few times, but maneuvering into the parking garage was awkward. A cop directing traffic gave me a warning because the right-side mirror was missing.

When we moved in 2001, I finally had a garage big enough for the Thunderbird. I bought a heavy-duty battery and found a mechanic who loved old cars. Then he moved away. I lost hope that I could do much with it. The great T-Bird became a temporary storage facility for clothes that were on their way to the bargain store. The grandchildren liked playing in it, because the battery still had enough juice to fire up the AM radio.

In February 2004, as I was waking up from open-heart surgery, one of my first thoughts was to donate the Thunderbird to a nonprofit. Then I argued with myself: *I can't give the car away. It was my dad's favorite toy. I won't have anything of his left. The car is rapidly deteriorating. Let it go. But to whom should I give it? Who has the know-how to handle the repairs?*

One year passed. Someone told me that if a car had been sitting for more than a year, it needed to be checked out by a mechanic. Which mechanic? A second year passed, then a third. The T-Bird never rolled an inch. It had given up and was content to live in the dirt, tied by cobwebs to a corner of the dark garage.

Finally I made a list of three nonprofits, and on my first call, the car was accepted by an enthusiastic director of a program for teenagers. "I have a connection at a Ford dealership who can handle the complications," he assured me.

One bright Saturday morning, the dealer sent a wrecker to pick up the old lady. There was yet another problem. The tires were flat, and Billy the wrecker man had no compressed air to resuscitate them. We found two carpenters, Pancho and Roberto, who were working down the street, and they helped us push. The Thunderbird resisted and held firm, her disintegrating tires sticking to the cement floor. Her power steering was now only Billy and me trying to turn the wheel.

The car finally gave way, and Billy pulled it up into the air onto the flatbed. Once there, the T-Bird seemed to change. With her low-cut lines and stately wheel covers, she looked majestic as she towered against the early morning sky. A brisk wind blew away her cobwebs and dried leaves. Her cream white surface seemed to radiate through the layers of grime. Her bleeding oil and the grave clothes of accumulated debris had been left on the cold garage floor. She was destined to fly, and she knew it. Alexandra and I saluted her and shed some unexpected tears as she soared away.

Fly, Bird of Thunder, fly!

It's Time! It's Time!

Funny things happen with time. Time flies, faster and faster with each passing year. No one seems to have enough of it, except perhaps for people in nursing homes, hospitals, and prisons. For them, time can creep.

Actually, time neither flies nor creeps; it never stops. It moves along like a stream, minute after minute, hour after hour, week after week. First, its Christmas, then New Year's, Easter, birthdays, the Fourth of July, the first day of school, and suddenly it's Christmas again.

The Greeks used two primary words for time: *chronos* and *kairos*. *Chronos* is ordinary time, a point or segment in time, all of it passing from one minute to the next. It is the river that keeps moving along.

Kairos is the word used for critical, fateful, or decisive moments. Every game, every battle, every life has its critical turning point. "You know how to interpret the appearance of the earth and sky," Jesus told a crowd of followers. "How is it that you do not know how to interpret this present time—this *kairos?*"[27]

I am at a place in my life that I am more comfortable with conventional time. I want the weather, the economy, the world political situation to keep more or less steady. While I give lip service to *kairos,* my psyche is more suited to *chronos*.

I have a young, impressionable friend who has been studying the Scripture with a group of people geared toward apocalypse.

27 Luke 13:5–6.

She tells me that, thanks to her new associates, she has read the Bible with understanding and excitement for the first time. "Listen to this," she tells me with wonder. "There is a time coming when wrong is going to be judged and punished, when tears are wiped away and faith small as a grain of mustard seed will be rewarded. That time is near. It's not going to be business as usual!"

I'm not thrilled by her interpretation. "Don't shake me up," I tell her. "God is faithful and regular." I've learned to live happily one day at a time, expecting to have twenty-four hours in which to eat, sleep, play, work, love, dream, and write. Each new day not much different than the next.

Still, I agree to take another look at Scripture. Of course, I discover I am right. Time is chronological, *chronos*. It rolls along, taking us through each week, through the seasons of the year and the seasons of life. There is a time to be born, and a time to die; a time to plant, and a time to pluck what is planted; a time to kill, and a time to heal, a time to laugh; a time to mourn.[28] The person who sets his or her internal clock to this natural rhythm of days and seasons will achieve a much more peaceful life than the person who ignores nature's cycles.

But the passionate young Bible student is also right. I discover in my Scripture reading another kind of time, *kairos*—a time that is full, complete, and decisive. When it comes, it roars. It was in *kairos* time that Jesus came the first time. "But when the fullness of time had come, God sent forth his Son, born of a woman."[29] Jesus says the arrival of this decisive time is like the arrival of an important person at our door when we least expect it. A king, a bridegroom, the owner.

28 Ecclesiastes 3:1–8.
29 Galatians 4:4.

My father once arrived at my door unannounced. Not so unusual, you say. But I lived in Florida, and he lived in Tennessee. He had something important to say, and I had to pay attention. The person who does not pay attention to these *kairos* times is going to miss them. Miss the party. Miss the wedding. Miss the boat.

And what a party! I don't want to miss it. Paul describes it like this: "Whatever we may have to go through now is less than nothing compared with the magnificent future God has planned for us. The whole creation is on tiptoe to see the wonderful sight of the sons of God coming into their own."[30]

The wise men noticed something was happening because they were watching the sky. Herod watched from his palace.[31] The shepherds watched from the hillside.[32] Anna, the holy woman, watched in the temple.[33] Even Ebenezer Scrooge didn't miss his *kairos* time.

In whatever way time passes for us, whether it flies, creeps, or just rolls along, it's time. Stop! Pay attention! Change direction! The kingdom of God is at hand.

30 Romans 8:18–19 (PHILLIPS).
31 Matthew 2:1–23.
32 Luke 2:8–20.
33 Luke 2:36–38.

What Is

I am at home, half in bed, half padding around the house. I picked up pneumonia or a flu on a trip to Brazil, and I get a little better, then I feel it coming back. People tell me to take it easy, but I don't want to. I want to be out reconnecting with friends in Atlanta and telling them about our experience in Brazil. This is taking too long. But that is not *what is*.

It is hard to live what is. I have often lived what was, what is to be, what I wish it was, or what it could have been. But how do I live what is?

Curitiba, Brazil: It's a dark and cold winter in southern Brazil. We arrive at the airport five minutes after our plane has taken off with our suitcases on board. Our host and hostess will meet the plane in an important interior town, and we will not be on it. They are influential state officials who were close friends of our friend Emmit Young, killed in Brazil a few years earlier. We do not have their phone number or access to a phone. They have arranged appointments for us in the morning. We have heard news reports saying that the president of Brazil will be there.

It doesn't matter that the ticket agent told me that the plane was late, that we had two extra hours. It doesn't matter that the plane made up the time and left on schedule. The last plane for the evening is gone. That is what is.

After some negotiations by our Curitiba host, the airline manager volunteers to hire a taxi. Off we go on a five-hour taxicab ride up mountains and down to the interior. By the time we arrive at the apartment of our hosts, it is 12:30 a.m., and I am not feeling well. I chill, then sweat. The people we have come to serve end up serving me—cooking soup for me, taking me to the doctor.

The next night we join our hosts for their family prayers and read the words of Isaiah. "They that wait upon the Lord shall renew their strength."[34] I feel humbled, like I pushed ahead of God. We could have spent a restful evening with our hosts in Curitiba. That is what was. What do I do now with what is?

Back in Atlanta, I'm in bed, sitting up. I hear a voice, not audible, but just as real: Tom, why not live what is? You have pneumonia even though you don't want it. Rest and make this time a retreat."

So Alexandra and I embark on an at-home retreat. We listen to the Gospels in Portuguese, then read Paul's letter to the Corinthians as if he's writing directly to us. Last evening Thomas Merton came to dinner, and Alexandra has lined up Dorothy Sayers, Henri Nouwen, T. S. Eliot, and I don't know who else.

This morning, we learned something from a conversation with E. Stanley Jones, a Methodist missionary and theologian who became friends with many leaders in India's independence movement, including Mohandas Gandhi. Jones was the founder of the Christian Ashram movement. He says that the root of the word *manna* is *what is*. (Manna was the food that the Israelites ate in the desert on exodus from Egypt.)

First Pilgrim: "What did you have for breakfast?"
Second Pilgrim: "What is." [35]

---

34 Isaiah 40:31.
35 E. Stanley Jones, *The Way* (Nashville: Abingdon Press, 1946), 229.

This morning I am not in my office calling friends and supporters, telling them about my trip to Brazil and all the wonderful things that the Atlanta Resource Foundation has done this year. I am not out and about, encouraging people to be partners in these efforts. I am at home on retreat, trying to live the only real way we can live: living with *what is*.

We've always got to live on what is. The children of Israel lived on manna in the wilderness. *Manna* means *What is*. They didn't know what it was, so they called it *What is*.

I was off loaded in Trinidad on my journey back by ship from South America, missing an important mass meeting in Miami. "I had a raw deal, Lord, I ask for power to take any treatment that may come and use it." Peace settled within me. You can live on *What is*, and the manna will feed you.

—E. Stanley Jones, Abridged from *The Way*

The Power of Two

"This is my position," she says.

"Well, I didn't hear you say that," I reply. "I heard something else."

We are having trouble hearing each other, but we are searching.

"This is what I mean," she says.

"Well, if that's what you mean, I certainly agree with you," I reply. "But that's not what I heard."

It's hard for either of us to let go. Finally, we zero in and agree. Alexandra and I are together on a particular issue facing us as a couple, but it took weeks to get there. Our unity, so difficult to achieve, is powerful. The children feel support rather than uneasy division. The basic family partnership, husband and wife, is together.

Jesus so believed in the power of a pair that he was willing to send out seventy green disciples, two by two, without money for food or lodging, to work against disease, sickness and evil. Evaluating their efforts, Jesus said, "I watched how Satan fell, like lightning out of the sky."[36] Agreement is such a powerful force, Jesus explained, "Where two or three are gathered together in my name, I am there in the midst of them."[37] He added the mysterious words, "Whatever you bind on earth shall be bound in heaven."[38]

But two is also complicated. It is not clear who is in charge.

36 Luke 19:18.
37 Matthew 18:20.
38 Matthew 18:18.

Between the two, they have to work out how they are going to operate. One summer, I teamed up with a Jamaican, Ed Chambers, who was living in the United States. Our plan was to go on a mission trip to Jamaica. I had been on similar trips already, but now there were two to decide who was going to raise the money, buy the tickets, plan the itinerary. There were two to find a place to stay and to decide what we would do each day.

Both of us were self-starters, and we were used to making decisions on our own. I wanted to drive and so did he. I wanted to see the pope, who was visiting Jamaica, and he didn't. Despite our disagreements, we did a lot of praying, discussing, waiting, and knocking on doors to see which one would open.

One hot afternoon we were trying to see an influential politician. We were not having much success finding his house. My snorkel gear was in the backseat, and the surf and the coral reefs were calling me. Ed was driving, and he was just about ready to give up and turn home, when I prayed, *Lord, if you want us to visit this man, put it in Ed's mind where his house is.*

In less than a minute, Ed made a U-turn and headed toward a back road. Before long we found the man at his farm. Once he learned that we were not hit men but friends of a friend, he began to relax. We had an excellent visit, and he agreed to invite some of his colleagues and friends over to begin building relationships with one another.

When two people have different ideas, agreement is not necessarily one person capitulating to the other's plans but a mutual discovery of a third way.

It is quicker to operate alone, and usually less expensive, but does it carry the power, insight, and backup capacity of two people? Dennis Pete, a longtime director of Urban Young Life in Atlanta, told me that some neighborhoods were becoming so dangerous that it was necessary to send leaders out in teams. The people doing dark deeds had teamed up in gangs. Why should the people doing good works be isolated?

When Emmit Young was killed in a head-on auto accident in Brazil, I lost my friend and my ministry partner. We knew each other's moves intuitively, and I felt lost. But I have since discovered that God gives me partners for different times, different places, and different types of service. It's not always the same person, but it's the same principle—two or three together agreeing. As a pair, we seem to be better able to plug into our unseen, but not-so-silent partner.

How Do You Say
"Stupid Talk-Show Host" in Spanish?

The people of faith have always been into language—from the tower of Babel to Pentecost to the New Jerusalem. Perhaps this is because we have a God who spoke (*dabar* in Hebrew), and there was the firmament, and the waters above were separated from the waters below. God spoke again, and animals and human beings were brought into existence. He even gave them names. This is language. Moses talked with God as a man talks with his friend, then wrote down what he heard. More language.

Language is so important that, at the tower of Babel, human beings tried to devise one language to make themselves even more powerful than they were. Fortunately, this experiment failed, and people have remained bi- and trilingual over most of history. Jesus probably spoke Aramaic, Hebrew, Greek, and a Galilean dialect. Even his unschooled fishermen disciples spoke at least two languages, and Pilate ordered the sign on the cross—Jesus, King of the Jews—to be printed in three languages. Pentecost itself was an outpouring of language.

In the first century, Greek was the language of the conquerors and remained so even under the Romans. French was the lingua franca of the eighteenth and nineteenth centuries, and English has become the language of the business world in the twenty-first century. It is important to learn English, particularly if you are answering tech calls from American customers. And if you are going to live in the United States, it would be best if you could speak and read English. It's not that English is a superior language, but it's convenient to have a common language in which to communicate.

But I do not understand the flap, the anger, and vengefulness of people, particularly talk-show hosts, who want every recent immigrant, whether legal or illegal, to learn English or get out! It would be far better if, while encouraging people to speak and read English, we learned a little of their language. Virtually every day in the United States we meet someone from another country who has learned to get by in English. Are we not just a bit ignorant if we don't take advantage of this living language laboratory? How do you say "stupid talk-show host" in Spanish?

I had my own moment of ignorance in the late 1950s, when the officers of my seminary shared a meal with the officers of a black seminary. These were the days in the South when the races did not mix or eat together. I learned over dinner that one of the black students spoke five languages, including French, German, and Italian. I was stunned, and my reaction only illustrates how isolated my culture had kept me.

Later, I lived overseas as a missionary. Our mission board sent us to language school. We made incredibly stupid, gross, hilarious errors, but the people were fascinated and helped us, and they wanted us to help them with their English. We all wanted to be bi- and trilingual. And, yes, we also knew something about prejudice against foreigners. It was the end of the sixties, and the world blamed us as Americans for our involvement in Vietnam and for most other troubles in the world.

My model is the late Manuel Bonnemaison, a Peruvian orthopedic surgeon who trained at the Mayo Clinic. I met him at a Latin America dinner in Washington, DC, and later he and his wife hosted Alexandra and me in their home in Lima. After he retired from a lucrative practice in Lima, Dr. Bonnemaison moved with his family to Washington. He became a treasured friend who gave me advice on cooking, diet and exercise, and keeping my marriage romantic. He loved people, and he had a good ear for language. When he met someone from another country, he quickly found out where they were from and started speaking to them in their own language. After he had run through basic greetings, he was pretty much reduced to "yes" and "no," but he made friends everywhere.

Manuel, for you I will welcome people to the United States by listening and learning to speak at least a few words in the language of their parents. Next time I'm at the checkout counter, I will ask, "How can I say 'Thank you' in your language?" When I travel to another country, I work hard to learn a little bit of the language before I go. It's a beginning.

I fantasize, Manuel, about organizing a group of Spanish speakers to flood the phone lines of a celebrated talk-show host. Each caller will politely ask, "Buenos dias, maestro estupido, porque husted no mi intendo?"

Laying August to Rest

August is a month of rest, or at least it used to be. For many people, it still represents the last weeks before the start of school. A time for one more trip to the beach or to the mountains. Quality family time. The last chance to rest until after Christmas.

August starts slow and lazy and then shoots like a Fourth of July rocket to Labor Day. I know the peaceful days of early August will give way to frenzy at the end of the month. It's August, I tell myself, and I am going to rest.

There is rest, but not as I expect.

First, there is the laying to rest of family members. People are not supposed to die in August. My brother-in-law's mom, Flossie Mitchell, makes it to her ninety-eighth birthday and then stops eating. She has always treated us like grandchildren, passing on sage advice, saying prayers for our family, and giving us Christmas tree ornaments that she made herself. Now she is gone.

My sister asks me to say a prayer at the graveside.

"Where is the cemetery?"

"Behind the Kroger's on Chapman Highway."

We drive the blue highways from the North Georgia mountains to Knoxville, noticing along the way that several stretches of highway are brown from construction.[39] It turns out that the cemetery is in *front* of the Kroger's. We lose valuable time trying to find our way. We arrive out of breath at the graveside just in time

39 The highways colored in blue on our maps represent the superhighways of yesteryear that have been bypassed by the interstate highway system. Once dotted with thriving commercial areas, they are now marked by decaying buildings, closed gas stations, antique shops, and cheap hotels.

to hear Flossie's preacher read, "Let not your hearts be troubled."

"She was a calming force to all who were rushing around," he says. He stops and looks anxiously at the gathering of friends and family.

"Is there a Thomas Roddy present?"

"Here." I raise my hand like a schoolboy. I move deftly and swiftly toward the casket, negotiating the narrow passageway between my surprised brother-in-law and the deep hole in the ground. I am able to be calm. I close with a peaceful, laying-to-rest prayer.

The next Monday it is Aunt Jan, my mother's sister-in-law, whose turn comes to be laid to rest. Having learned our lesson, we arrive ninety minutes early at a beautiful church, St. John's Episcopal, in downtown Knoxville. It is not far from where my mother grew up with her brother and sister, Jim and Elizabeth. Aunt Jan was Jim's wife. She had a radiant smile and flashing eyes and could see the best in the worst situations. She had been the youngest of her generation, and now she was the last to go.

I am not expecting my tears. It must be the magnificent liturgy, the sounds of a trumpet, and the sight of my three cousins and their children. We sing together the closing hymn, "Now the Day Is Over," the same hymn my cousins sang to their mother at night in the nursing home: "Now the day is over, night is drawing nigh, shadows of the evening steal across the sky."

The third to go is Celestine Sibley, the beloved reporter and columnist who worked for the *Atlanta Constitution/Journal* from 1944 until her death on August 15, 1999. I only talked with her twice, but she wrote like we were family. She is eulogized in my home church, but I stay in my "sweet apple" log cabin in the Georgia mountains, reading some of her columns and crying—for the generation that is gone and for three ladies who endured pain and loss but kept the faith, each in her own unique style. I weep for the nearness of the time when our day is over.

At the end of August, instead of rushing toward September, I am in a cath lab, resting on a gurney and then a table. I watch the screen while a doctor works wonders with wires to open up the arteries in my left leg. August is gone. Fall is here. I have not gotten the rest I am looking for but the one I need. And I have new legs.

Throughout the fall, each night as I lay my head on my pillow, a lullaby-like hymn runs through my mind. I've learned something from my aunt Jan. There is a rest that I do not have to wait for until August comes again. One night, I kneel by my grandson's bed and sing the hymn as best I can. He is just learning his numbers. He tells me that I will die, " 'cuz you can't live to eighteen eighty." He goes to sleep.

> Jesus give the weary
> Calm and sweet repose
> With Thy tenderest blessings
> May mine eyelids close.
>
> Comfort those who suffer
> Watching late in pain
> Those who plan some evil
> From their sin restrain.
>
> When the morning wakens
> Then may I arise
> Pure and fresh and sinless,
> In Thy holy eyes.[40]

---

40 "Now the Day Is Over," Sabine Baring-Gould, 1867.

When the Well Runs Dry

Friendship in a Time of
Global Economic Collapse[41]

The war creates no absolutely new situation: it simply
aggravates the permanent human situation so that we
can no longer ignore it. Human life has always been
lived on the edge of a precipice. Human culture has
always had to exist under the shadow of something
infinitely more important than itself. If human beings
had postponed the search for knowledge and beauty
until they were secure, the search would have never
begun. We are mistaken when we compare war to
"normal life." Life has never been normal.

—C. S. Lewis, "Learning in Wartime," 1939

It's been seventy years since C. S. Lewis gave his famous lecture,
"Learning in Wartime," at Oxford University, addressing the
question of how to justify academic pursuits when civilization
stood at the brink of destruction. Today those of us who are
in helping professions must ask ourselves the same hard questions. What does it mean to be a "resource foundation" when
the resources have dried up? How shall we continue to be in

41 This reflection is adapted from a talk I gave in 2009 at the twenty-fifth anniversary of
the Atlanta Resource Foundation. Many foundations whose major role is grant making
were wringing their hands about the global downturn. Their endowment income had
dried up, and their reason for existence was badly curtailed. The resources of the
Atlanta Resource Foundation, however, are people, friends, connections, and brave new
ideas—and they were never more needed.

the caring business when we have fewer and fewer resources to express our care? Should a hospital with no medicine stay open?

For me, at least part of the answer to these questions is found in friendship. There is no better time to learn how to befriend ourselves and other kindred spirits and even to be a friend of God. Here are some guidelines I've found helpful, using the word *friends* as a memory enhancer.

> **Feed** ourselves. In the mornings, I read my Bible, and before I do that, I listen to great music or read the thoughts of inspiring writers. I make a point of being with people who feed my faith, who are positive and uplifting. Especially now, I don't need negative friends. I refuse to listen to talk shows that drag me down, and I don't watch the market all the time. (There is a fine line between *informed* and *panicked*.) I give thanks for the sun and the wind and the rain. I'm more in touch with the seasons, take more walks, enjoy sunsets.

> Get **Real** with ourselves, with God, with one another. A friend shared with me his spiritual journey as he convalesced from valve replacement surgery. On some days, as dusk approached, he became anxious, and as the darkness crept in, he grew more fearful. I experienced something similar after my own heart surgery, and I sometimes asked people to stay with me. Since then, for three years, I have been in a support group for people with a history of heart problems. I have never once heard anyone admit to being afraid at night that they would not live to see the light of day. Adults are not supposed to be afraid of the dark. As

part of my commitment to honesty, when a friend asks me how I am, I pause for a moment to think about how best (and concisely) to respond. It's one small way I can develop friendships that are based on reality and that are mutually encouraging and sustaining.

Avoid **Isolation**. Even if we're embarrassed because we're dragging the bottom, we cannot retreat to bed. We need to get to bed—and out of bed. In the past my exercise was solitary. I liked to be alone with my own thoughts. I still like this from time to time, but more and more I seek out exercise where I can be with others. A friend cannot help me if I'm hiding, and while I still believe in silver linings, I've learned that it can be dangerous and unhealthy to ignore the storm.

Empathize with ourselves and one another. "Come alongside us," the empathic ones say. We are all in the same boat. Silver and gold have we very little in an economic disaster, but we can do this or that. I can be your friend. Isn't that the miracle of the gift of the Spirit? Jesus told his followers that he would be with them even after his death, when the Spirit, the "one who comes alongside," was present to them.

Act **Now**. Don't wait for a better tomorrow, because it may not come. Don't stop giving of your financial resources, even if you can't give as much as you've given in the past. To people and organizations in need, it is not much consolation to hear, "I might be able to give in two or three years." Can we give some encouragement today?

Embrace **Difficult** times as friends and teachers.
For eleven years, the Atlanta Resource Foundation
shared space with other small, brave nonprofits in a
pre–Depression era office building reluctantly owned
by North Avenue Presbyterian Church in Atlanta.
We had air conditioning in the winter and hot air
in the summer. They were hard times, but many
of us came of age there. We were far closer to one
another in those years than after we changed to an
upscale uptown office building—where there was
no likelihood of heatstroke or frostbite, and every
night some invisible person emptied our trash and
vacuumed the rugs. We were friends because of our
shared difficulties, not in spite of them.

Speak. Honor, applaud, celebrate, bless. Find those
who are doing good and support them. Some will
do better than you have done. Some may even take
your ideas and act like they are theirs. Celebrate them.
Without being religious, by speaking the right words at
the right time, you can be a means of divine blessing
to your family, friends, and community.

Now with fear and trembling I amend the words of C. S. Lewis:
If human beings had postponed the search for friendship and
encouragement until they were secure, the search would have
never begun.

The Place That God Reveals

> Go from your country and your kindred and your
> father's house to the land that I will show you.
>
> —Genesis 12:1

Greg Simmons was a man ahead of his time. He wrote in his
journal when most of us thought journaling meant working for
a newspaper. He learned to paint in oils when we thought painting was not a hobby for men. (When he told his wife, Christie,
that he wanted to paint, she gave him a bucket of paint and a
roller.) He even finagled a way to conduct the Atlanta Symphony
Orchestra.

Greg read books on beekeeping and the works of C. S.
Lewis before either were popular. He bought a place in the
mountains of western North Carolina before anyone thought
of buying a second home outside the city. Who needed a farm
in the mountains?

Greg gave a lot of thought to young, hard-driving businesspeople who lived their lives completely separate from the
church. He thought they could be challenged to face the social
issues of the city if they could sit face to face with people who
were enduring homelessness and unemployment, addiction and
mental illness.

Greg was our risk taker. Once he had received 51 percent
support for an idea, he jumped in. We called his modus ope-
randi, "Fire, ready, aim." It was only after he died that I learned
he was shy and had a problem with stuttering.

Although he was not an academic, Greg sat on my dissertation committee when I was getting my doctor of ministry degree from Columbia Theological Seminary. One afternoon, just as I was wrapping up my seminary education, Greg called me.

"I have an idea. When you finish your degree, let's start a foundation!"

Greg always had ideas. But another foundation?

"Just what the world needs," I told him.

"This one will be different," Greg explained. "We won't give money, and we won't give grants. Money always gets in the way of relationships."

By that time Greg was an extraordinarily successful young businessman, and he knew a lot about the damaging power of money. Our foundation's capital would come in the form of relationships. If we could build friendships throughout the city, the assets would flow to where they were needed whether they passed through us or not.

"We won't create our own projects," Greg added. "We will just hang out, be available, try to figure out where the Spirit is working in the city, and encourage and support these works."

That was how the Atlanta Resource Foundation was born. Greg and Christie printed all our stationery and paid for our logo. This was my ministry home for over twenty-five years. We never kept score by referring to our balance sheet, and sometimes Greg's idea was sorely tested. What really were we doing?

One beautiful spring day, when Greg was only forty-two, he fell from the top of a waterfall to his death. He had been leading four of his five children on a hike up a mountain. The oldest was only twelve; the youngest, who had stayed at home, was only two. His death took our breath away, devastating not only his immediate family but his friends and the entire community of Atlanta. Surely God had made a terrible mistake.

But now I think maybe Greg was just once again going ahead of us. Although he has been gone almost a quarter of a century, I figure he is still helping us out, challenging us to take risks, strengthening us to be bold, to think out of the box.

"Let's be like Abraham," I can still hear Greg say. "Let's go the place that God will reveal."

Epilogue

Most people, including me, need a physical **home** to have an emotional and spiritual **home**. So a lot of my life's work has focused on helping others create places of shelter, safety, and identity—a **home**.

But sometimes it is hard to get there.

I am heading home from a visit with my editor in Stone Mountain, Georgia, and I more or less know the way. But since there are a few turns I'm not familiar with, I ask my GPS navigation to take me home. That polite but authoritative lady—I am sure you have heard her voice—keeps trying to take me off the freeway and onto secondary roads.

"Exit immediately and turn right."

"But that's not the way I want to go," I answer. "You can't be correct. I'm going to follow my intuition, not your directions."

It isn't until I get home that I realize that the lady isn't wrong; she is just doing what she has been told. I have accidentally checked the "Do not allow freeways" icon. I make a mental note: be clear about the instructions you give yourself when you are trying to get home.

In 1992, I go home to Tennessee to be with my father who is celebrating his ninetieth year. My mother died eleven years earlier. Dad is living mainly in an upstairs bedroom and in the kitchen, which now serves as the den, the living room, and the TV room. My mother's steaming pots have been replaced by an aluminum frying pan and a toaster oven. In the corner is a Sony portable television with rabbit ears.

The room we used as a den, with its warm paneling, is cold. The worn furniture is hidden by the white slipcovers my mother had made for those hot summer days before air conditioning. We used to gather here as a family to listen to show tunes and to watch girls in fantasia costumes performing in big studio productions. During the cold winter nights of World War II, we listened to Walter Winchell broadcasting nightly news reports from London.

The home I knew as a child is just a memory.

Feeling homesick and bereft, I rummage around an old chest of drawers and find one of my mother's old Bibles. It falls open at a bookmarker. There I read a verse that my mother had underlined.

"The kingdom of God cometh not by observation...
for, behold, the kingdom of God is within you."[42]

It is as if she has just left these words of Jesus there for me to read. I have spent a lot of time praying and working for the kingdom of God to come and searching outwardly for signs of its arrival. Now I understand more clearly that the kingdom is within, the gift of God. The journey home, the journey to God, is a journey within my own heart.

Home really is where the heart is.

42 Luke 17:20–21 (KJV).

Wandering Home

And when I am home with myself
There are some trails I have not noticed.
There are other paths to explore, some roads not taken.
I do not have to go around the same old circle again,
Safe within the ruts that I have grooved for myself.

Frodo Baggins, the ring bearer, the hero of J. R. R.
Tolkien's epic saga,
could have returned to his home in the Shire.
Even made it into a model hobbit village
With his three friends.
But he chose another road
One that took him to a new Home over the Sea.

As Frodo walked along with his buddy Sam
He sang an old walking song with new words:

> Still round the corner there may wait
> A new road or secret gate;
> And though I oft have passed them by,
> A day will come when I
> Shall take the hidden paths that run
> West of the Moon, East of the Sun.

I will choose a new route, and new routes will be chosen for
me. My guide promises to be with me on the untried way.